Horst Hegewald-Kawich

Dogs from A to Z

- ➤ Favorite Dog Breeds from All Over the World
- ➤ Extra Feature: How to Find the Right Puppy

BARRON'S

Contents

Breed Groups

Dog Sketches

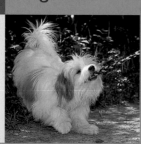

Choosing a Dog

Appendix

Breed Groups

There are at least 300 breeds registered with the FCI (the Federation Cynologique Internationale), the international umbrella organization for dog breeders. They are divided into eleven groups. Some of the breeds in this book are totally foreign to American soil but their history is significant to many dogs common to the United States and other countries.

Group 1
Sheepdogs and
Cattledogs (except
Swiss Cattledogs)

When humans settled
down and began raising
livestock, they protected
their herds from predators
with large **guard dogs.**
When the flocks of sheep
became larger, the pastures
became smaller, and people
needed medium-sized,
nimble, resourceful, and
easily trained guard dogs
that quickly learned how to
keep the sheep out of the
cultivated fields. Since
wolves had essentially been
exterminated by that time,
the powerful guard dogs
were out of work. Fortu-
nately, those wonderful
herd protectors still exist
in various breeds in southern
and eastern European
mountain regions, as well
as in Siberia.

Herding dogs are generally easy to train and adapt
well to humans. They are
intelligent, often sensitive,
and ordinarily submissive
and alert. Though they tend
to chase wild game, with
consistent training they can
be taught just about any-
thing. Large livestock
breeders, butchers, and
cattle dealers needed tough,
courageous dogs for their
own protection and for
herding the livestock—the
so-called **herding dogs,** of
which Rottweilers are representative. Many cattle
dealers made the collars of
their Rottweilers in such a
way that they could conceal
all of their masters' money.
A thief would have had to
kill the dog in order to get
the money.

Group 2
Pinschers, Schnauzers,
Molossians (ancestor of
the Mastiff), and Swiss
Mountain- and Cattledogs

Pinschers generally include
small, smooth- or coarse-

**Typical body language
of a Border Collie while
herding sheep.**

Herd protectors can be good family dogs.
Herd protectors have been changed and today many are
excellent companions for active people who understand the
herding mentality and enjoy providing gentle and consistent
training. Shepherd dogs generally fit harmoniously into the
family and are intelligent, useful companion dogs when gentle
training methods are used.

haired dogs. Formerly they were referred to as "ratters," for their main purpose was to get rid of rats in the barn-yard and the animal stalls. They were not allowed to roam, and despite their desired watchfulness, they were not vicious. The German Spitz, which has nothing in common with the Nordic Spitz, is the classic watchdog among the house and yard dogs.

Dogs that look fearful because of their frightening configuration, massive body and head, powerful fangs, long ears, and impressive size, belong to the **Molossian breeds**. These powerful house and yard defenders have common forebears in the Tibetan Mastiffs, and

Jack Russells are always eager to work underground.

they spread worldwide through the Assyrian **Molossians**. These dogs belong mainly in the hands of people who understand the breeds. The **Swiss Mountain Dogs** are useful farm dogs. Entlebuchers and Appenzellers, in addition to their value as watchdogs, were used as good, nimble herders; on the other hand, Bernese Mountain Dogs and Great Swiss Cattledogs (see photo on page 7) served well for guarding and performed service as draft dogs.

Group 3
Terriers

No matter which Terrier breed we deal with, heart, intelligence, and vitality are common to them all. They often tend toward tenacity and independence. That makes them capable of attacking a fox or a badger in its burrow, and flushing it

The wirehaired Dachshund looks out at the world with confidence.

out of its tunnel in front of the hunter's gun. This is also the source of their name: *terra* = earth, thus *Terrier*. Their job was to combat vermin in the field and meadow, and hunt rats and mice. They performed the tasks with a passion. All Terrier breeds are good companion dogs as long as the handler is more persistent than the dog.

badgers and foxes in their burrows. Thus, they evince a strongly independent nature that many people wrongly take for stubbornness.

Group 4
Dachshunds

Just like the short-legged Terriers, this breed was originally intended for hunting

Group 5
Spitzes and Primitive Dogs

Spitz-typed dogs were probably the oldest form of domestic dog. In northern regions, the Spitz is used for hunting, pulling sleds, and

EXTRA TIP

Terriers — Special Dogs
With Terriers everything is special: they are vital, confident, independent, animated, daredevil, intelligent, crafty, pugnacious, active, playful, stubborn, strong-willed, fond of hunting, task-oriented, quick to learn, action-loving, plus cuddly, loyal, and devoted.

If you like all these qualities in a dog, then you are the ideal partner for a Terrier — except for the Hunting Terrier, which you should leave to the hunters.

herding, but in other countries it is used more as a watchdog and companion. The Japanese hunting dogs such as the Akita are part of the Spitz family. The ringed tail, the more or less stocky, square body, the high hindquarters, the pointed fangs, and pointed, erect ears are characteristic of their configuration. From breed to breed, though, there are very significant differences in temperament.

Dogs regarded as belonging to the ancient breeds include the Canaan Dog, Pharaoh Hound, Mexican and Peruvian Hairless, and the Basenji. Ancient breeds for hunting include the Canary and Ibiza-Podenco, the Cirneco dell'Etna, and the Portuguese Podengo. These greyhound-like hunting dogs, which formerly

EXTRA TIP

Spitzes Love to Hunt
German Spitzes are not particularly interested in hunting. Hunters are especially fond of the Wolf Spitz because it has a wild nature. All northern Spitzes are among the most enthusiastic hunters of all the breeds, and they thus present some problems for people who want to walk with their dogs off lead.

were referred to as Mediterranean Greyhounds, hunt with their nose as well as with their eyes.

Group 6
Scent Hounds and Related Breeds

Scent hounds follow the trails of large game with great passion and persistence, and hunt in packs or singly with a hunter. They bark loudly on the trail. Hunters affectionately refer to this as the *baying* of their dogs.

The Podenco hunts and retrieves rabbits.

As time went on, both the hunting methods and the hunter's armament changed. So hunting dogs had to be bred for specific purposes. The so-called leaders of the pack, which worked the trail of the wild game with the pack, were no longer needed. They were

> **In some countries fox hunting with hounds is no longer permitted.**

used to breed the highly talented **hunting dogs** that are capable of finding wounded game. Their continuous barking informs the hunter of their location.

EXTRA TIP

Primitive Dogs

The dogs included in this FCI breed category are justifiably called primitive. Dog lovers with a taste for the uncommon get a covetous look in their eyes when they encounter such dogs. These are always special dogs, with interesting, beautiful conformation or especially primitive behavior. Only true connoisseurs should take on such a dog, provided they are able to fully satisfy the dog's high demands.

Running free and following trails in fields and meadows is the specialty of hunting dogs.

game, point, retrieve, and are tough enough to offer the hunter a measure of protection.

The Irish Water Spaniel, a water dog with water-repellent fur.

Group 7
Pointing Dogs

With the advent of firearms, people began to raise **Pointing Dogs.** These dogs announce the location of game by lifting a foreleg and staring ahead without moving. When the hunter approaches within shooting distance, the dog flushes the game on command so that the hunter can shoot. The dog must not only be accustomed to gunfire, but must also fetch and return the downed game to the hunter without damaging it (retrieving). In the type of game farm hunting that is sometimes practiced today, versatile dogs are called for; they search for and flush the

Group 8
Retrievers, Flushing Dogs, and Water Dogs

All Retriever breeds in Group 8 are hunting specialists, the **Retrievers.** Their

> EXTRA TIP
>
> **For Hunters Only**
> Almost all Scent Hound breeds in Group 6 and all Pointers in Group 7 are outstanding hunting dogs and are appropriate mainly in the hands of hunters. Their breed-specific task orientation is quite strong and some are hard to satisfy with other exercises such as dog sports.

A retriever's favorite job is bringing back the dummy.

name is descriptive of their main task: finding and fetching game. They are active, medium-sized, powerful, and compactly built dogs that generally retrieve with a "soft mouth," that is, without damaging the game. They like the water even in winter. They are quite good as companion dogs, as long as they get exercise through dog sports as a substitute for their hunting activity. Among the **Flushing Dogs** the various Spaniel breeds predominate.

The German Spaniel is the only exception. Spaniels, regardless of specific breed, are used increasingly as companion dogs, much like Dachshunds. This is also true for the **Water Dogs**, of which the Irish Water Spaniel is a typical representative. Hunting for waterfowl is their passion. In the house they are easy to manage and very intelligent. They are very uncommon,

13

Bred to be "smiling" companions to their humans.

so there is cause for concern over the continuation of the breeds. Dogs used for hunting may have their tails docked as a safety measure.

Group 9
Companion and Toy Dogs

Because of their social skills and their tremendous adaptability, these dogs are capable of being valued companions to humans in modern civilization. In size they range from miniature to medium-sized dogs. Their fur is not always suited to a specific purpose, and is mainly attractive, but in many cases it also requires lots of care. There are some dogs that have no hair at all aside from a meager tuft on top, and so they need to be protected with sunscreen. Many breeds elicit sympathy among dog lovers, who feel that these dogs are "abused." In this group we find all the

Sighthounds hunt with their eyes, whereas other hunting dogs use their nose.

breeds that have no task other than pleasing their owners with their presence. And they do this with great adaptability. But this also makes them particularly sensitive. Behavioral idiosyncrasies such as independence and decreased trainability are found among certain bloodlines of purely companion dogs.

Group 10
Sighthounds

In contrast to the other hunting dogs, the nose plays a minor role with these visual hunters. These run-

ning hounds are the oldest form of hunting dogs. Formerly they were referred to as hunting hounds, swine dogs, and other terms. Their ancestors evidently came from the broad steppes of Asia or the desert regions of the Near East and Africa. Their physique alone shows that they were bred for speed: tall, sinewy legs, slender torsos with arched backs. A deep, voluminous thoracic cage provides the lungs and heart with plenty

---

EXTRA TIP

Criteria for a Companion Dog
Desirable qualities are an even disposition, trainability, moderate hardiness, close bonding, good focus, and a willingness to fetch and play.

The dog may also have qualities as a watchdog and defender.

Undesirable traits include anxiety, shyness, excessive mistrust, pugnacity, and strong hunting instinct.

Every companion dog should be able to demonstrate its suitability to the purpose.

of room. Running and hunting are the most important things to them. Chasing after an artificial hare is a necessary but poor substitute for these dogs' inherent hunting need. Every animal that moves quickly can trigger this hunting drive and will ultimately be caught if the greyhound is not restrained on a leash. In such situations the dog is no longer focused on its owner's commands. By nature they are mysterious, sensitive, noble, and affectionate personalities. People who love these beautiful dogs must carefully consider if they can meet their needs a hundred percent. If not, they should refrain from owning this type of dog.

Some places have strict laws governing fighting dogs such as Pit Bulls.

EXTRA TIP

FCI Group 11
This group includes breeds whose breeding associations have filed for recognition with the FCI and have been accepted provisionally. Such cases include the Australian Shepherd (see page 42) and the White Swiss Shepherd (see page 224). Their eventual recognition as a breed is surely imminent.

The Behavior of So-called Fighting Dogs

There are a number of limitations that face owners of fighting dogs (dogs with pronounced aggressiveness and that pose safety risks). Since such dogs often are considered dangerous, some areas have laws that require special registration. These laws are not uniform, and different breeds may be considered fighting dogs, so before acquiring such dogs, potential owners should become familiar with special local ordinances. Often a muzzle

> **Many mongrels are fond of playing in water.**

and a leash are required for these dogs in public places. When traveling to another region or country, owners should inquire about laws pertaining to dogs.

Potential owners of these dogs would be wise to check with their insurance company regarding liability coverage in the event their dog causes harm to people and/or property.

EXTRA TIP

Mongrels

Many dogs are mutts or mongrels that fill pounds and shelters in every city. Mutts are attractive to some owners because many are as intelligent as purebreds and display hybrid vigor (heterosis) which gives them an added measure of good health, lack of the hereditary diseases, and personality quirks of purebreds. These dogs are destroyed by the millions every year and most would make good pets if given half a chance.

Technical Terms of the FCI

➤ **Affinity**
Inherent attraction, kinship, or interest in another.

➤ **American Kennel Club**
Abbreviated AKC, this organization acts as a registry of almost 140 recognized dog breeds. It provides pedigree information and breed "standards."

➤ **Bat Ear**
Erect ear, wide at the base, with rounded tip (e.g., French Bulldog).

➤ **Bloodline**
Complete information about a dog's ancestors.

➤ **Blue Merle**
Bluish striping in fur.

➤ **Brand**
Light, regular markings in darker fur of a dog (e.g., Rottweiler).

➤ **Breeding**
Intentional union of male and female dogs of the same breed to produce puppies with desired traits inherited from the parents.

➤ **Breeding Certificate**
Statement of a dog's worthiness to breed.

➤ **Breed Group**
Presentation of at least three dogs from the same kennel at a show. The individual dogs must be judged at least *good* on the same day in the individual evaluations.

➤ **Bristle Hair**
Harsh, medium-long, rough hair that sticks out only a little.

➤ **Build**
Dog's physique; conformation.

➤ **Button Ear**
High set ears that fall toward the front and lie close to the head.

➤ **CAC**
Abbreviation for "Certificat d'aptitude au championnat." Contention for a national championship title.

➤ **CACIB**
Abbreviation for "Certificat d'aptitude au championnat international de beauté." Contention for international beauty championship.

➤ **CACIT**
Abbreviation for "Certificat d'aptitude au championnat international de travail." Contention for international work championship for work dogs.

➤ **Championship**
Winning title for dogs that come closest to goal for breed.

➤ **Chipping**
Inserting a computer chip under the dog's skin; in conjunction with a reading device, this allows checking the dog's identity.

➤ **Cocked Ear**
With high tipped ears or folded ears only the upper tip folds forward (e.g., Collie). With severely cocked ears, the upper third tips forward (e.g., Fox Terrier).

➤ **Conformation Rating**
Evaluation of how close a dog comes to its breed standard. Examples: exceptional, very good, good, adequate, inadequate.

➤ **Constitution**
Inherited physical qualities and physical capabilities, independent of breed, sex, and external factors.

➤ **Cross Breeding**
Mating between breeds.

➤ **Croup**
Rear portion of a dog's back from the last lumbar vertebra to the start of the tail; composed of sacrum, both hips, and overlying muscles.

➤ **Cynology**
Science of the dog. From the Greek *kyon,* dog, and *logos,* teaching.

➤ **Dewclaw**
Atrophied fifth toe located on the legs above the paws. With many breeds (e.g., Bauceron), dewclaws on hind legs are addressed in the breed standards.

➤ **Dewlap**
Loose skin under the throat (e.g., St. Bernard).

➤ **Domestication**
Taming of wild animals and breeding for use and companionship by humans.

➤ **Dominant Trait**
Visible hereditary factor that suppresses other inherited characteristics.

➤ **Dorsal Stripe**
Small stripe of darker hairs along the spine.

➤ **Double Coat**
Wolf-like hair consisting of medium-long topcoat with

thicker undercoat (e.g., German Shepherd).

➤ **Dry**
Term applied to muscular dogs with tight skin and no layer of fat.

➤ **Family Tree**
Equivalent to genealogical tree.

➤ **Feathers**
Long hair on legs, ears, and tail.

➤ **Flag**
Long hairs on underside of tail.

➤ **Flanks**
Soft parts between ribs and upper leg.

➤ **Folded Ears**
Also button ears. Ears attached high on head, falling to the front and lying close to the head.

➤ **Guard Hair**
Coarse hairs covering the undercoat.

➤ **Heat**
Bitch's breeding time, approximately every six months.

➤ **Hind Quarters**
Hind legs, thighs, and hips.

➤ **Markings**
Different-colored spots in the dog's coat.

➤ **Mask**
Usually dark pigmented part of a dog's head around the muzzle or on skull.

➤ **Muzzle**
Dog's snout up from the stop to the end.

➤ **Passing Gait**
Simultaneous forward movement of both legs on one side of the body.

➤ **Pedigree**
Information on a dog's parentage issued by breed registry office; also referred to as a family or genealogical tree; phylogenetic tree.

➤ **Phenotype**
A dog's physical conformation.

➤ **Pigmentation**
Coloration in nose speculum, edges of lips, and rims of eyelids.

➤ **Purebred**
Exhibiting breed specific traits inherited from homozygous parents.

➤ **Recessive**
Opposite of *dominant*. Recessive traits are stored inside the genotype and reappear in later generations.

➤ **Registry Book**
Directory of all dogs bred in a breed category.

➤ **Retrieving**
Fetching objects and wild game, usually on command.

➤ **Rose Ear**
The backside of the ear is folded inward so that the inside of the ear canal is visible. The tip points downward (e.g., English Bulldog).

➤ **Rough Hair**
Short or medium-long topcoat that sticks out in different directions and feel harsh and rough (e.g., Rough- or Wirehaired Dachshund).

➤ **Salt and Pepper**
Dark topcoat with light tips (e.g., Schnauzer).

➤ **Standard**
Description of the ideal type of a breed published by the breed association in the country of origin.

➤ **Stop**
Step between skull and nose bone.

➤ **Striped**
Containing dark stripes on lighter fur, as with a Boxer.

➤ **Tan**
Designation for yellow to rust brown, as with Black and Tan Terrier.

➤ **Tattooing**
Placing an embossed identification number inside the ear or on the inner thigh using a tattooing instrument and dye.

➤ **Trimming**
Plucking out dead hairs to maintain an even, standard prescribed shape of the dog (e.g., Airedale Terrier).

➤ **Trousers**
Long, soft hairs on underside of dog's upper leg.

➤ **Tulip Ear**
Tulip-shaped erect ears (e.g., German Shepherd).

➤ **Undercoat**
Soft, woolly, fine hairs under a dog's guard hairs (winter fur).

➤ **Wirehair**
Short, stiff hair.

➤ **Withers (also shoulder height)**
Located between the shoulder blades. Reference point for measuring a dog's height.

Dog
Sketches

The 200 most beloved dog breeds
arranged by their FCI names are
presented in sketch form. Each
breed includes history, character,
and living conditions, as well
as brief information about
appearance and suitability.

Explanation of the Sketches

(on pages 28–227)

Breed Name: This includes the breed as recognized by the Fédération Cynologique Internationale (FCI).

Also: Other common names for this breed.

History: The history of the breed with respect to breed origin, original breeding goal, and present-day usage.

Character: The most important features and behavior traits of the breed in question, its conduct in the home, and with regard to strangers and other dogs.

Living Conditions: The conditions that should exist for the given breed to feel at ease.

Health: Diseases that may crop up in particular breeds. For Illnesses from A to Z, see pages 246 through 249.

Appropriate for: Carefully evaluate your knowledge and experience with dogs.

Brief Info: Here you will find the FCI group to which the breed belongs. In addition you will find information on the country of origin, size, weight, fur and coat color, and life expectancy.

Data Box: Ownership requirements at a glance. The number of "paw prints"(1 through 5) indicates the following:

➤ **Training:** The harder a breed is to train, the more paw prints.

➤ **City:** The less suited a breed is for life in a city, the more paw prints. A *no* means that the breed is inappropriate for the city.

➤ **Family:** The more paw prints a breed has, the less likely it is to integrate into a family.

➤ **Care:** The more intensive the care required by the breed, the more paw prints.

➤ **Activity:** The more paw prints, the greater the need to keep the dog appropriately occupied. The various dog sports are important substitutes.

Technical terms of the FCI are explained on pages 18 through 21.

Chart Clarification

On pages 26 and 27 you will find fifty breeds grouped according to the categories "Dogs for Beginners" (page 26) and "Dogs for Advanced Owners/Specialists" (page 27). In this context, a beginner in dog ownership is someone who has little

> **The active Tervuren needs athletic involvement.**

experience. Advanced owners/specialists have experience with various breeds and are used to dealing with the particular qualities of individual breeds.

In the House: Appropriateness for keeping in an apartment, or suitability only for living indoors.
✔ = poorly suited
✔✔ = moderately suited
✔✔✔ = well suited
No = unsuited

Fitness: The requirement of providing a dog with breed-specific activities.
✔ = little demand
✔✔ = medium demand
✔✔✔ = high demand

Care: The demand for care such as trimming.
✔ = little demand
✔✔ = medium demand
✔✔✔ = high demand

FOR BEGINNERS

BREED	PAGE	IN HOME	FITNESS	CARE
Australian Shepherd	42	✔✔	✔✔✔	✔
Bearded Collie	50	✔✔	✔✔✔	✔✔✔
Bernese Mountain Dog	56	no	✔	✔✔
Cairn Terrier	73	✔✔✔	✔✔✔	✔✔
Cavalier King Charles Spaniel	76	✔✔✔	✔	✔✔
Cocker Spaniel	83	✔✔	✔✔	✔✔✔
Collie (Longhair)	84	✔✔✔	✔✔✔	✔✔
Dachshund	89/90	✔✔✔	✔✔	✔
Dalmatian	91	✔✔✔	✔✔✔	✔
English Springer Spaniel	99	✔✔✔	✔✔✔	✔✔
Eurasier	101	✔✔✔	✔✔	✔✔
German Boxer	108	✔✔✔	✔✔✔	✔
Golden Retriever	117	✔✔✔	✔✔✔	✔✔
King Charles Spaniel	140	✔✔✔	✔	✔✔
Kromfohrlander	143	✔✔✔	✔✔	✔
Labrador Retriever	145	✔✔✔	✔✔	✔✔
Landseer	148	no	✔✔	✔✔
Miniature Schnauzer	162	✔✔✔	✔✔	✔✔✔
Newfoundland	165	no	✔✔	✔✔✔
Old English Sheepdog	170	✔✔	✔✔	✔✔
Poodle	159/211	✔✔✔	✔✔	✔✔✔
Shetland Sheepdog	201	✔✔✔	✔✔✔	✔✔
Spitz	208/209	✔✔	✔✔	✔
West Highland White Terrier	221	✔✔✔	✔✔	✔✔✔
Yorkshire Terrier	227	✔✔✔	✔✔	✔✔✔

FOR EXPERIENCED OWNERS/SPECIALISTS

BREED	PAGE	IN HOME	FITNESS	CARE
Afghan Hound	29	✔	✔✔✔	✔✔✔
Airedale Terrier	30	✔✔✔	✔✔✔	✔✔
Akita Inu	32	✔✔✔	✔	✔
Alaskan Malamute	33	no	✔✔✔	✔
Beauce Shepherd	51	✔	✔✔✔	✔
Berger de Brie	53	✔	✔✔✔	✔✔✔
Border Collie	62	✔✔	✔✔✔	✔
Chow Chow	81	✔✔✔	✔	✔✔✔
Doberman	94	✔✔✔	✔✔✔	✔
English Setter	98	✔✔	✔✔✔	✔✔✔
German Mastiff	111	✔✔	✔	✔
German Shepherd	112	✔✔	✔✔✔	✔
German Shorthair	113	✔✔	✔✔✔	✔
German Wirehair	115	✔✔	✔✔✔	✔
Giant Schnauzer	116	✔✔	✔✔✔	✔
Gordon Setter	118	✔✔	✔✔✔	✔✔
Irish Setter	128	✔✔	✔✔✔	✔✔
Irish Wolfhound	132	✔✔	✔✔✔	✔
Kuvasz	144	✔✔	✔	✔✔
Malinois	154	✔✔	✔✔✔	✔
Parson Jack Russell Terrier	173	✔✔✔	✔✔✔	✔
Rhodesian Ridgeback	188	✔✔✔	✔✔✔	✔✔
Rottweiler	189	✔✔	✔✔✔	✔
Saint Bernard	191	no	✔	✔
Siberian Husky	204	no	✔✔✔	✔

Affenpinscher

History: People who feel that character is more important than good looks will make a good choice in an Affenpinscher. Probably the product of a Belgian Griffon and a rough-haired Pinscher, this dog began as a rat and mouse exterminator.

Training: 🐾 🐾
City: 🐾
Family: 🐾
Care: 🐾 🐾
Activity Level: 🐾 🐾

Character: Very affectionate and dependent on its humans. Toward strangers it appears to be a testy but earnest watchdog. With careless training it may become domineering. An intelligent, tough litle dog that is quick to learn. Overall, a big personality.

Living Conditions: An ideal indoor dog because of its size. Easy to care for, with minor trimming of body hair. With normal supervision behaves fine with older children, but will not accept being abused as a plaything.

Health: Physically robust dog, rarely ill.

Appropriate for: Beginners

QUICK INFO FCI Group 2/No. 186: *Pinschers and Schnauzers, Molossians, Swiss Mountain Dogs* **Country of Origin:** *Germany* **Size:** *10–12 inches (25–30 cm)* **Weight:** *8.8–13.2 pounds (4–6 kg)* **Fur:** *hard, thick, and abundant* **Color:** *predominantly black, brown or gray markings are acceptable* **Life Expectancy:** *15 years and older*

Afghan Hound

Also: *Afghan Greyhound*

History: In its homeland it was accustomed to hunting all kinds of game. Afghans are found in many homes today. Breeding began in some western countries only in the thirties; recently the fur has become fuller through breeding with American dogs, and the dog has become more of a status symbol.

Training: 🐾 🐾 🐾 🐾
City: 🐾 🐾 🐾 🐾 🐾
Family: 🐾 🐾 🐾 🐾
Care: 🐾 🐾 🐾 🐾 🐾
Activity Level: 🐾 🐾 🐾 🐾 🐾

Character: Training requires patience and sensitivity. Afghans are proud and dignified; blind obedience is not their thing. They are aloof and reserved and sometimes remain distant with their owners.

Living Conditions: Running free is out of the question, so a large, fenced-in yard is required so the dog can run around. Directed exercise is necessary.

Health: Corneal degeneration, glaucoma, elbow dislocation, hip dysplasia (HD).

Appropriate for: Experienced dog owners

QUICK INFO FCI Group 10/No. 228: Greyhounds **Country of Origin:** *Afghanistan* **Size:** *males 25–29 inches (64–74 cm), females 24–28 inches (60–70 cm)* **Weight:** *males 44–55 pounds (20–25 kg), females 33–44 pounds (15–20 kg)* **Fur:** *long, silky* **Colors:** *all colors* **Life Expectancy:** *14 years and more*

Airedale Terrier

Formerly: *Bingley Terrier*

History: This is a cross involving the Otter Hound, Bull Terrier, Gordon Setter, and Black and Tan Collie. Its originator, Wilfried Holmes from the English county of Yorkshire in the dale of Aire, created a multifaceted, dashing, and weatherproof dog. In the last two World Wars the Airedale proved itself in medical and dispatch service.

Character: Spirited, easy to train, motivated to learn, alert, with good qualifications as a watchdog. Can be a real clown right into old age and provide lots of enjoyment to a family.

Living Conditions: Always wants to be in on everything and needs tasks to perform, which it gladly takes on. With gentle training, it becomes an enthusiastic partner in dog sports. The fur requires trimming every twelve weeks.

Health: HD, possible muscle tremors.

Appropriate for: Experienced owners

Training: 🐾
City: 🐾 🐾 🐾
Family: 🐾
Care: 🐾 🐾 🐾
Activity Level: 🐾 🐾 🐾 🐾 🐾

QUICK INFO FIC Group 3/No. 7: *Terriers* **Country of Origin:** *Great Britain* **Size:** *males 23–24 inches (58–61 cm), females 22–23 inches (56–59 cm)* **Weight:** *around 44 pounds (20 kg)* **Fur:** *wiry, hard, thick* **Color:** *tan with black or grizzled saddle, neck, and top of tail* **Life Expectancy:** *up to 15 years*

Akbash

History: This is one of the most handsome and unspoiled herding dogs. Its well-balanced, harmonious physique and pure white, thick fur give it a very elegant appearance. It is still used mainly in the region west of

Training:	🐾 🐾 🐾 🐾
City:	🐾 🐾 🐾 🐾 🐾
Family:	🐾 🐾 🐾 🐾 🐾
Care:	🐾 🐾
Activity Level:	🐾 🐾

Ankara for herding. Supposedly all white European herding dogs are descended from the Akbash. In the United States this breed is used successfully for herding.

Character: Like all herd protectors, this dog is accustomed to working and making decisions independently. When it's in action, it hears no further commands. Anything that belongs to its herd is totally under its protection.

Living Conditions: As a typical herding dog, this is not the best choice for a companion dog.

Health: Very vital, with lots of endurance.

Appropriate for: Very experienced owners

QUICK INFO FIC Group: *Not recognized* **Country of Origin:** *Turkey* **Size:** *males 30–34 inches (76–86 cm), females 28–32 inches (71–81 cm)* **Weight:** *male about 119 pounds (54 kg), females 90 pounds (41 kg)* **Fur:** *double-coated or long hair* **Color:** *pure white* **Life Expectancy:** *around 8 years and longer*

Akita Inu

History: The center for Akita breeding is still located in the Akita prefecture. Akita-type dogs go back five thousand years in Japan. Around 1900 the Akita was used primarily as a hunting and work dog. It retains its passion for hunting.

Training: 🐾 🐾 🐾
City: 🐾 🐾 🐾 🐾
Family: 🐾 🐾 🐾
Care: 🐾 🐾 🐾
Activity Level: 🐾 🐾 🐾

Character: Proud, often resolute. With close family bonding, which it needs, it is calm and dignified. Resists force in training. Tends toward role reversal with trainers.

Living Conditions: Currently used only as a companion dog. Its equanimity has limitations, however. Because of its passion for hunting and its dominant behavior toward other dogs of the same sex, the Akita must be kept under strict control.

Health: HD, skin and hair problems, autoimmune system disorders, epilepsy, progressive retinal atrophy.

Appropriate for: Experienced owners

QUICK INFO FIC Group 5/ No. 255: *Spitzes and Primitive Dogs* **Country of Origin:** *Japan* **Size:** *males 26 inches (67 cm), females 24 inches (61 cm), give or take an inch (3 cm)* **Weight:** *66–88 pounds (30–40 kg)* **Fur:** *double-coated, thick with undercoat* **Color:** *red, white, sesame, brindle (streaked)* **Life Expectancy:** *up to 14 years*

Alaskan Malamute

History: The largest and strongest of the sled dogs. Its name comes from the Mahlemuts, a native Alaskan people from the region where it originated. It is no sprinter, but an endurance puller. In European latitudes this beautiful dog is out of place, but it fares well in northern locales.

Training: 🐾 🐾 🐾 🐾
City: 🐾 🐾 🐾 🐾 🐾
Family: 🐾 🐾 🐾
Care: 🐾 🐾
Activity Level: 🐾 🐾 🐾 🐾 🐾

Character: Friendly to strangers. Although it is calm and composed, it can spring into action like lightning. With other, smaller animals it needs to be watched carefully. The Malamute is very attached to its human.

Living Conditions: Like all Nordic dogs it needs a clear definition of its role in the family. Even in the winter it loves to be active outdoors. It tolerates heat poorly and needs contact with active people.

Health: HD, dwarfism, hereditary kidney disease.

Appropriate for: Experienced owners

QUICK INFO FIC Group 5/No. 243: *Spitzes and Primitive Dogs* **Country of Origin:** *United States* **Size:** *males 25 inches (64 cm), females 23 inches (59 cm)* **Weight:** *males 86 pounds (39 kg), females 75 pounds (34 kg)* **Fur:** *medium long, harsh with thick undercoat* **Color:** *all colors with acceptable light markings* **Life Expectancy:** *over 12 years*

American Bulldog

History: English Bulldogs came to America along with the British settlers. The farmers crossed them with other breeds, using no unified standard, to develop a reliable dog to protect home and livestock and help with herding.

Training: 🐾 🐾
City: 🐾 🐾 🐾 🐾
Family: 🐾
Care: 🐾
Activity Level: 🐾 🐾

Character: Sturdy, unobtrusive family dog. Even though it is also a bit strong-willed, it is quite trainable. Very alert, with no pronounced aggressiveness.

Living Conditions: Likes to have a house and yard, preferably with "live inventory" that it can look over and patrol. Adequate exercise with interactive games keep it even-tempered.

Health: Hip dysplasia (HD), problems with bone development, joint problems. With pure white strains, watch out for possible partial or complete deafness and/or blindness.

Appropriate for: Experienced owners

QUICK INFO FIC Group: *Not recognized* **Country of Origin:** *United States* **Size:** *males 23–28 inches (58–71 cm), females 20–24 inches (51–61 cm)* **Weight:** *males 90–150 pounds (41–68 kg), females 70–130 pounds (32–59 kg)* **Fur:** *short hair* **Color:** *pure white, red spotted, brown, cream, striped on white background* **Life Expectancy:** *12 years and older*

American Cocker Spaniel

History: One of the most beloved dog breeds, the Cocker Spaniel was bred from the English Cocker Spaniel. It is not often used for hunting.

Training: 🐾🐾
City: 🐾
Family: 🐾
Care: 🐾🐾🐾🐾🐾
Activity Level: 🐾🐾🐾🐾

Character: This is a merry, affectionate family dog that is easy to train. It desires close contact with its humans. A good watchdog, but not a barker. With good obedience training its hunting instinct is controllable.

Living Conditions: In comparison to the English Cocker Spaniel (see page 83), it has a luxuriant coat that requires a lot more care. Because of its need for contact, this is not a dog that simply runs along with the family.

Health: Eyes: progressive retinal atrophy (PRA), cataracts; Skin: allergies; sebaceous gland disorders, pustules in jowl area; HD.

Appropriate for: Beginners

QUICK INFO FIC Group 8/No. 167: *Retrievers, Flushing Dogs, and Water Dogs* **Country of Origin:** *United States* **Size:** *males 15 inches (38 cm), females 14 inches (35.5 cm)* **Weight:** *22–26 pounds (10–12 kg)* **Fur:** *soft, abundant, and full* **Color:** *one-colored: black, cream to dark red and brown; multi-colored: black and white, red and white, brown and white, mottled, blotches of black and other colors* **Life Expectancy:** *up to 15 years*

American Staffordshire Terrier

History: Under the name of Staffordshire Bull Terrier, this dog arrived in North America along with British immigrants. Only later did it acquire its present name. Under the name Pit Bull Terrier (*pit* referring to the dog fight arena) it is bred in the United States and elsewhere for pets, but sometimes is used as pit fighters.

Training: 🐾🐾🐾
City: 🐾🐾🐾🐾
Family: 🐾🐾🐾
Care: 🐾
Activity Level: 🐾🐾🐾🐾🐾

Character: Like all classical breeds of fighting dog, the "Staff" with responsible breeding and AKC (American Kennel Club) papers is harmless and impartial with people. It is spirited and quick to learn.

Living Conditions: Ample socialization with other dogs and animals from the earliest age on is absolutely necessary. This self-assured dog needs lots of leadership training.

Health: HD.

Important Note: Check into laws regulating dangerous dogs (see page 16).

QUICK INFO FIC Group 3/No. 286: *Terriers* **Country of Origin:** *United States* **Size:** *males 18–19 inches (46–48 cm), females 17–18 inches (43–46 cm)* **Weight:** *37–44 pounds (17–20 kg)* **Fur:** *Short hair* **Color:** *all colors, white over 80 percent, black and tan and liver color undesirable* **Life Expectancy:** *up to 15 years*

American Water Spaniel

History: As the name indicates, this dog is suited for water tasks. Apparently it was the product of crossing Retrievers and English and Irish Water Spaniels. An outstanding swimmer, this dog also has a good nose and is an expert in waterfowl and marsh birds.

Training: 🐾
City: 🐾 🐾 🐾 🐾 🐾
Family: 🐾
Care: 🐾 🐾
Activity Level: 🐾 🐾 🐾 🐾

Character: A friendly and even-tempered dog in the house, but not overly fond of children. A good watchdog, but not particularly aggressive.

Living Conditions: These water dogs have a water-resistant, curly coat that traps air. They are excellent at retrieving and thrive on regular work that requires an abundance of interactive exercise.

Health: HD, progressive retinal atrophy.

Appropriate for: Hunters

QUICK INFO **FIC Group 8/No. 301:** *Retrievers, Flushing Dogs, and Water Dogs* **Country of Origin:** *United States* **Size:** *15–18 inches (38–46 cm)* **Weight:** *males 30–45 pounds (13.5–20.5 kg), females 25–40 pounds (11.5–18 kg)* **Fur:** *water resistant, curly hair that traps air and forms an undercoat* **Color:** *chocolate brown, leather brown; small, white markings on feet and chest are acceptable* **Life Expectancy:** *10 to 15 years*

Appenzeller Cattle Dog

History: This old Swiss farm dog breed is a jack-of-all-trades. It watches attentively over house and yard, barking at strangers. It herds the cows back from the pasture by nipping them on the hocks; it may do the same thing, although much more lovingly, with playful children. Aside from its traditional jobs, this dog is seen as an enthusiastic participant (barking all the time, of course) in other activities, and it is nimble in negotiating agility obstacles.

Training: 🐾🐾
City: 🐾🐾🐾🐾🐾
Family: 🐾
Care: 🐾
Activity Level: 🐾🐾🐾🐾🐾

Character: Lively, vital, alert, very self-assured. Incapable of lazing around and always looking for things to do.
Living Conditions: Should be kept in homes with big yards. It needs either its traditional jobs or active, athletic, adventurous people.
Health: No common illnesses.
Appropriate for: Beginners

QUICK INFO FIC Group 2/No. 46: *Pinschers and Schnauzers, Molossians, Swiss Cattle Dogs* **Country of Origin:** *Switzerland* **Size:** *males 20–22 inches (52–56 cm), females 19–21 inches (50–54 cm)* **Weight:** *44–66 pounds (22–30 kg)* **Fur:** *short, thick, shiny* **Color:** *black with symmetrical rust-brown and white markings* **Life Expectancy:** *up to 15 years*

Argentine Mastiff

Also: *Dogo Argentino*

History: Starting around 1900 the Dogo Argentino was bred from a mixture of various Spanish mastiffs, Bull Terriers, and Pointers. It soon became evident that the Dogo, which had been intended as a pure hunting dog for puma, jaguar, and wild boar, could also be used for police and military work. The breed was recognized in 1973 as the only Argentine dog breed to date.

Training: 🐾 🐾
City: 🐾 🐾 🐾 🐾 🐾
Family: 🐾 🐾 🐾 🐾
Care: 🐾
Activity Level: 🐾 🐾 🐾 🐾 🐾

Character: This dog has very good qualities as a watchdog and protector, and is very courageous. With early, consistent training it is an easily managed companion.

Living Conditions: This dog should fit into indoor living very well, but it needs an experienced handler.

Health: Deafness, HD, cleft palate.

Appropriate for: Experienced owners

QUICK INFO FIC Group 2/No. 292: *Pinschers and Schnauzers, Molossians, Swiss Mountain Dogs* **Country of Origin:** *Argentina* **Size:** *males 24–27 inches (62–68 cm), females 23–26 inches (60–65 cm)* **Weight:** *84–110 pounds (38–50 kg)* **Fur:** *short guard hairs with no undercoat* **Color:** *pure white, dark flecks on head acceptable, black nose* **Life Expectancy:** *10 to 12 years*

Australian Cattle Dog

History: The British colonists were quick to find out that the Collies they brought with them were not tough enough for herding the huge cattle herds in the heat. So they created their Australian Cattle Dog by cross-

Training: 🐾 🐾
City: 🐾 🐾 🐾 🐾 🐾
Family: 🐾 🐾
Care: 🐾
Activity Level: 🐾 🐾 🐾 🐾 🐾

ing their short-haired Blue Merle Collies with indigenous Dingoes, and later on with Bull Terriers and Dalmatians. This dog has great endurance, robustness, nimbleness, and hardiness.

Character: This dog is continually alert and has a strong protective instinct. It is a very courageous and loyal defender. It is quick to learn, but needs consistent training.

Living Conditions: This dog is happiest outdoors. In Australia it is a beloved family dog. However, it always wants to work, play, and practice sports with its family. It won't be content with a low-energy lifestyle.

Health: PRA and deafness occasionally occur.

Appropriate for: Knoweldgeable and constant owners

QUICK INFO **FIC Group 1/No. 287:** *Sheepdogs and Cattledogs* **Country of Origin:** *Australia* **Size:** *males 16–20 inches (40–51 cm), females 17–19 inches (43–48 cm)* **Weight:** *35–44 pounds (16–22 kg)* **Fur:** *short, hard* **Color:** *blue or red flecked* **Life Expectancy:** *9 to 12 years*

Australian Kelpie

History: The Kelpie is to working with the huge Australian sheep herds as the Cattledog is to cattle ranchers. It was bred from the shorthaired Scottish Collie. In 1872, when a female named Kelpie from this new sheepdog breed won the first national herding championship, all its descendents became referred to as Kelpies.

Training:	🐾
City:	no
Family:	🐾 🐾 🐾 🐾
Care:	🐾
Activity Level:	🐾 🐾 🐾 🐾 🐾

Character: An eager but even-tempered dog passionately devoted to work. When it wants to get around sheep, it simply runs over their backs. It works very independently in the herd.

Living Conditions: The Kelpie is happiest in situations where there is plenty of activity including dog sports, but it also likes family living. Its temperament and desire to work require experienced owners.

Health: Scarcely any hereditary diseases.

Appropriate for: Knoweldgable owners

QUICK INFO **FIC Group 1/No. 293:** *Sheepdogs and Cattledogs* **Country of Origin:** *Australia* **Size:** *males 18–20 inches (46–51 cm), females 17–19 inches (43–48 cm)* **Weight:** *35–44 pounds (16–22 kg)* **Fur:** *short* **Color:** *black, black-tan, red-tan, chocolate brown, smoky blue* **Life Expectancy:** *around 10 years*

Australian Shepherd

History: When shepherds immigrated to America from other countries they often brought their sheepdogs with them from their native lands. Dogs with Dingo and Collie blood arrived along with the Australian sheep imports. The Australian Shepherd evolved from all these dog breeds.

Training:	🐾
City:	🐾 🐾 🐾 🐾
Family:	🐾
Care:	🐾 🐾
Activity Level:	🐾 🐾 🐾 🐾 🐾

Character: A powerful dog with great endurance and temperament, friendly toward people, patient and gentle with other animals. A good watchdog with protective instinct. Learns quickly and easily. Does not tend to chase wild animals.

Living Conditions: This spirited and hardworking dog needs exercise and tasks to perform. A good family dog that fits in and accepts its role in the family as long as it gets appropriate activity.

Health: HD and deafness in merle colored dogs.

Appropriate for: Beginners

QUICK INFO FIC Group 11/No. 342: *provisionally accepted breeds* **Country of Origin:** *United States* **Size:** *males 20–22 inches (50–57 cm), females 17.5–21 inches (45–52.5 cm)* **Weight:** *29–44 pounds (13–22 kg)* **Fur:** *medium long, luxuriant* **Color:** *blue-merle, red-merle, red with or without white and copper-colored markings* **Life Expectancy:** *12–15 years*

Australian Silky Terrier

History: This breed arose at the start of the nineteenth century from a cross between a rough-haired Terrier bitch and a Dandie Dinmont Terrier. English breeder Mr. Little later crossed the Australian Terrier and a Yorkshire Terrier. That produced the steel blue, silky-haired Australian Silky Terrier.

Training: 🐾
City: 🐾
Family: 🐾 🐾
Care: 🐾 🐾 🐾
Activity Level: 🐾 🐾 🐾

Character: An intelligent, uncomplicated housedog that is content and easy to train. Despite its small size, it remains a Terrier that's ready to tackle any rodent. This dog doesn't appreciate small children who are loud and boisterous.

Living Conditions: Needs close family contact and lots of activity. Although the silky hair doesn't shed, it requires regular care.

Health: A very robust breed. Possible cryptorchidism, kneecap dislocation, kidney stones, diabetes.

Appropriate for: Beginners

QUICK INFO **FIC Group 3/No. 236:** *Terriers* **Country of Origin:** *Australia* **Size:** *9 inches (23 cm)* **Weight:** *7.5–10 pounds (3.5–4.5 kg)* **Fur:** *very fine and straight, but not reaching the ground* **Color:** *blue-tan color* **Life Expectancy:** *up to 20 years*

Australian Terrier

History: As early as the start of the seventeenth century, Scottish settlers in Australia were using small, rough-haired Terriers as incorruptible watchdogs and pest eradicators. The ancestors were various English Terrier breeds.

Training: 🐾
City: 🐾
Family: 🐾
Care: 🐾 🐾 🐾
Activity Level: 🐾 🐾 🐾 🐾 🐾

Character: This dog is always busy with something. Watchful, but not a barker. A robust adventurer, but friendly with people and other animals. Happy and devoted, it is easy to train even though it is very self-assured.

Living Conditions: This self-assured dog becomes an obedient comrade with consistent training and understanding of the Terrier nature. Its adaptability makes it a good family dog. It is athletic and has good endurance.

Health: This dog doesn't like cold weather. PRA, diabetes, and cryptorchidism occur rarely.

Appropriate for: Beginners

QUICK INFO **FIC Group 3/No. 8:** *Terriers* **Country of Origin:** *Australia* **Size:** *about 10 inches (25 cm)* **Weight:** *14.5 pounds (6.5 kg)* **Fur:** *hard, straight, with soft undercoat* **Color:** *blue with tan (puppies are black at birth)* **Life Expectancy:** *14 years and over*

Azawakh

History: A quick, independent hunter that is also used for watching over the herds of the nomadic Touareg peoples in the southern Sahara. The origins of the Touareg culture and their dogs are lost in history.

Training: 🐾 🐾 🐾 🐾
City: no
Family: 🐾 🐾 🐾
Care: 🐾
Activity Level: 🐾 🐾 🐾 🐾 🐾

Character: Very lively, and still spontaneous and energetic. Generally somewhat reserved. But anyone the Azawakh gives its heart to has its love forever after.

Living Conditions: As a type of greyhound it needs lots of appropriate exercise. As long as this is provided on a daily basis, it will fit in nicely as a housedog. Roughness in training will harm the dog. The main requirements are knowledgeable understanding, patience, and love.

Health: As long as the dog is cared for properly, there are no common diseases.

Appropriate for: Experienced owners

QUICK INFO **FIC Group 10/No. 307:** *Sighthounds* **Country of Origin:** *Mali* **Size:** *males 25–29 inches (64–74 cm), females 25–27 inches (60–70 cm)* **Weight:** *males, 44–55 pounds (20–25 kg); females 33–44 pounds (15–20 kg)* **Fur:** *short, fine* **Color:** *sandy to brown of all kinds from yellow to red, white markings and black mask acceptable* **Life Expectancy:** *10–12 years*

Basenji

History: According to Egyptian sources, the Pharaohs had Basenji-like dogs four thousand years ago. Some of them still exist in places such as Zaire and the Sudan in the so-called primitive state. The only dog of this kind living in that region to be recognized as a breed is the Basenji. It is used as a hunting dog.

Training: 🐾 🐾 🐾 🐾
City: 🐾 🐾 🐾 🐾
Family: 🐾 🐾 🐾
Care: 🐾
Activity Level: 🐾 🐾 🐾 🐾 🐾

Character: This dog does not bark, but rather emits a kind of yodel, which doesn't sound aggressive. It grooms itself like a cat and is absolutely odor-free. Intelligent, unobtrusive, and playful. It has a tremendous hunting instinct.

Living Conditions: It needs loving contact with its humans, who must exercise lots of patience with training, since it tends to have a mind of its own.

Health: Eye troubles, anemia, kidney stones, metabolic disorders, allergies to chemicals. Females come into heat only once a year.

Appropriate for: Experienced owners

QUICK INFO FIC Group 5/No. 43: *Spitzes and Primitive Dogs* **Land of Origin:** *Central Africa* **Size:** *16–17 inches (40–43 cm)* **Weight:** *20–24 pounds (9–11 kg)* **Fur:** *short, silky* **Color:** *red and white, black and white, black, white, and tan (tricolor), streaked* **Life Expectancy:** *about 13 years*

Basset Hound

History: Basset Hounds were originally bred for hunting in nearly impenetrable thickets. For some time breeding stressed anatomy to the extent that even the character of this fantastic dog began to resemble its caricature. Sensible breeding is slowly gaining the upper hand.

Training: 🐾🐾🐾
City: 🐾
Family: 🐾
Care: 🐾🐾
Activity Level: 🐾🐾🐾

Character: Independent and self-assured, which sometimes borders on stubbornness. Affectionate, very devoted, patient with children, and friendly with other dogs and animals.

Living Conditions: Not particularly gifted in running because of its physical build. Trained with consistency and patience, an acceptable family dog, but which still needs supervision.

Health: The anatomy produced by breeding leads to many joint and bone problems, which in turn cause further illnesses. Hopefully this beautiful dog will respond to better breeding practices.

Appropriate for: Beginners

QUICK INFO **FIC Group 6/No. 163:** *Scent Hounds and Related Breeds* **Country of Origin:** *Great Britain* **Size:** *13–15 inches (33–38 cm)* **Weight:** *40–55 pounds (18–25 kg)* **Fur:** *short, smooth, thick* **Color:** *all known dog colors* **Life Expectancy:** *8 to 12 years*

Bavarian Mountain Hound

History: The breed owes its pure breeding to the need of Bavarian high mountain hunters for a dog that will work hard while hunting, hunt loudly, and announce the death of the game by barking. It tenaciously follows the blood trail of wounded game. This dog was bred from the old Bavarian Bracke and the Hanoverian Bloodhound. Its tenacity made it an essential helper for professional hunters in the old days of poaching. Strict breeding choices and conscientiousness in providing puppies only to hunters are exemplary practices.

Training: 🐾
City: 🐾 🐾 🐾 🐾 🐾
Family: 🐾 🐾 🐾 🐾 🐾
Care: 🐾
Activity Level: 🐾 🐾 🐾 🐾 🐾

Character: A wonderful hunter and dependable searcher. Very strong work ethic. A gifted climber in the mountains.
Living Conditions: This dog is appropriate only for hunters.
Health: No particular illnesses known.
Appropriate for: Hunting specialists

QUICK INFO FIC Group 6/No. 217: *Scent Hounds and Related Breeds* **Country of Origin:** *Germany* **Size:** *18–20 inches (45–50 cm)* **Weight:** *around 66 pounds (30 kg)* **Fur:** *short, thick, somewhat rough* **Color:** *every shade of red and dark red, also with black hair tips* **Life Expectancy:** *13 years and longer*

Beagle

History: One of the oldest breeds of scent hounds, the Beagle was used mainly in packs for hunting rabbits and hares. The breed has been known since the fourteenth century. In contrast to the practice with larger pack dogs, hunters with Beagles hunt on foot rather than on horseback.

Training: 🐾 🐾 🐾
City: 🐾 🐾 🐾
Family: 🐾 🐾 🐾 🐾 🐾
Care: 🐾
Activity Level: 🐾 🐾 🐾

Character: Very adaptable, friendly toward people and other dogs. It also bonds equally with children. It is very playful and always ready for training and play.

Living Conditions: Training must begin early, otherwise the Beagle will become overly independent. Its good nose, which it used to follow every track, and its gluttony are its only drawbacks.

Health: Eye diseases such as glaucoma and cataracts, PRA; tendency to develop problems with ligaments.

Appropriate for: Beginners

QUICK INFO **FIC Group 6 /No. 161:** *Scent Hounds and Related Breeds* **Country of Origin:** *Great Britain* **Size:** *13–16 inches (33–40 cm)* **Weight:** *26–33 pounds (12–15 kg)* **Fur:** *short, smooth, thick, not very fine* **Color:** *orange, white, black, tan, tricolor* **Life Expectancy:** *12 to 15 years*

Bearded Collie

History: Originally a shaggy, weather-proof sheepdog in the Scottish highlands, now it's one of the best-groomed and most noticeable show and family dogs. With its current fur, which demands lots of care, it is less suited for herding.

Training: 🐾
City: 🐾 🐾 🐾 🐾
Family: 🐾
Care: 🐾 🐾 🐾 🐾 🐾
Activity Level: 🐾 🐾 🐾 🐾 🐾

Character: A friendly, spirited, and perpetually happy dog. It is very sensitive and frequently is distracted by noise.

Living Conditions: Cannot stand harsh training. Training must, however, be consistent. This dog needs lots of variety and exercise in its activity.

Health: Relatively free of hereditary diseases. Sensitive skin, with insufficient care. It should be fed relatively high-quality food.

Appropriate for: Beginners

QUICK INFO **FIC Group 1/No. 271:** *Sheepdogs and Cattledogs* **Country of Origin:** *Scotland* **Size:** *20–22 inches (50–56 cm)* **Weight:** *about 66 pounds (30 kg)* **Fur:** *long, double with soft undercoat and straight, hard, shaggy top coat* **Color:** *slate gray, fawn, black, blue. White blaze, white on tip of tail, on throat, on legs and paws* **Life Expectancy:** *12 to 14 years*

Beauce Shepherd

Also: *Beauceron, Berger de Beauce*

History: A very old type of French shepherd, which is also a reliable protector of the herd. In the Middle Ages it was used for hunting wild pigs. Its talents as a police and customs dog are increasingly valued.

Training: 🐾 🐾
City: no
Family: 🐾 🐾 🐾
Care: 🐾
Activity Level: 🐾 🐾 🐾 🐾 🐾

Character: A strong-nerved, tough dog with inborn focus and defensiveness. Because of its exceptional nature, it needs adequate socialization and gentle, consistent training.

Living Conditions: This self-assured dog needs plenty to do even in civilian life, especially when it has a chance to use its nose.

Health: HD, the dew claws (see page 19) prescribed in the Standard have no purpose and are prone to injury.

Appropriate for: Experienced owners

QUICK INFO **FIC Group 1/No. 44:** *Sheepdogs and Cattle-dogs* **Country of Origin:** *France* **Size:** *males 24–28 inches (65–70 cm), females 24–27 inches (61–68 cm)* **Weight:** *66–84 pounds (30–38 kg)* **Fur:** *short double coat* **Color:** *black and red (bas-rouge = red stockings) or harlequin (gray, black, and red)* **Life Expectancy:** *11 to 13 years*

Bedlington Terrier

History: Originally this dog was used for rat control by the English miners in the area around Bedlington. The following very different breeds may have been in the gene pool: Bull Terrier, Rough-haired Terrier, Greyhound, Otter Hound, and Bulldog. Nowadays this is purely a companion and show dog.

Training:	🐾 🐾
City:	🐾
Family:	🐾 🐾
Care:	🐾 🐾 🐾 🐾 🐾
Activity Level:	🐾 🐾 🐾

Character: Inside, it is still like a terrier: alert, quick, tough, and tenacious on varmints. Unfortunately, some Bedlington Terriers are said to be shy. You should watch closely for that fault when buying a puppy.

Living Conditions: This dog needs plenty of attention, and from its earliest days on it needs ample socialization. It does not always appreciate children.

Health: Copper toxicosis (inability to metabolize copper), retinal dysplasia, inherited kidney disease.

Appropriate for: Beginners

QUICK INFO **FIC Group 3/No. 9:** *Terriers* **Country of Origin:** *Great Britain* **Size:** *16 inches (41 cm)* **Weight:** *17.5–23 pounds (8–10.5 kg)* **Fur:** *fine, frizzy, cottony* **Color:** *blue and tan, blue and sand* **Life Expectancy:** *up to 15 years*

Berger de Brie

Also: *Briard*

History: One of the oldest French shepherds, it has long been without a herd to protect. Now it is kept almost exclusively as a companion dog. This is the longhaired version of the Berger de Beauce (see page 51).

Training: 🐾 🐾 🐾
City: no
Family: 🐾 🐾
Care: 🐾 🐾 🐾 🐾 🐾
Activity Level: 🐾 🐾 🐾 🐾 🐾

Character: Outwardly spirited, moody, and watchful, but sometimes tends to be resolute.

Living Conditions: Highly intelligent, this dog is a quick learner but is strongly independent and wary of strangers and other dogs. It is very trainable when consistency and gentleness are used. It needs daily walks for exercise and frequent grooming.

Health: Hypothyroidism, PRA, HD, and renal dysplasia are occasionally diagnosed.

Appropriate for: Experienced owners

QUICK INFO **FIC Group 1/No. 113:** *Herding and Guard Dogs*
Country of Origin: *France* **Size:** *males 24–27 inches (62–68 cm), females 22–25 inches (56–64 cm)* **Weight:** *around 66 pounds (30 kg)* **Fur:** *long, frizzy, slightly wavy, thick insulating coat* **Color:** *black, gray, dun, without white markings*
Life Expectancy: *10 to 12 years*

Berger de Picardie

Also: *Picardie Shepherd*

History: Even though this is an old breed, this rough-haired French shepherd is very rare. It has the same type of history as the Briard and the Beauceron (see pages 51 and 53).

Training: 🐾 🐾
City: 🐾 🐾 🐾 🐾 🐾
Family: 🐾
Care: 🐾
Activity Level: 🐾 🐾 🐾 🐾 🐾

Character: With close bonding to the family, this dog is calm and composed in the house. It is patient with children, and reserved with strangers. It is alert without being vicious, and it is a reliable watchdog. Outdoors it shows its true colors: it has speed, agility, and endurance.

Living Conditions: This is an ideal sports dog and companion for active people. Since it was bred to act independently as a shepherd, it often asks "why?" during training. Its behavior is practically problem-free.

Health: Very robust and rarely ill.

Appropriate for: Beginners

QUICK INFO FIC Group 1 /No. 176: *Sheepdogs and Cattle-dogs* **Country of Origin:** *France* **Size:** *males 24–26 inches (60–65 cm), females 22–24 inches (55–60 cm)* **Weight:** *62–77 pounds (28–35 kg)* **Fur:** *rough, weatherproof* **Color:** *gray, gray and black, gray with black luster, gray and blue, reddish gray* **Life Expectancy:** *10 to 12 years and longer*

Berger des Pyrénées

Also: *Pyrenees Shepherd*

History: For hundreds of years, this easygoing sheepdog has been driving herds in the mountainous regions of the Pyrenees, while its colleagues, the powerful Pyrenees Mountain Dogs, protected them from wolves.

Training: 🐾 🐾 🐾
City: 🐾 🐾 🐾 🐾 🐾
Family: 🐾 🐾 🐾
Care: 🐾
Activity Level: 🐾 🐾 🐾 🐾 🐾

Character: Very dependent, loyal to only one master, unerring, and alert. Often quick-tempered and not particularly easy to train. Its courage makes it a watchful defender.

Living Conditions: If a person can't offer this energetic, lively, and self-assured dog enough activity, it may become despondent and obstinate. When you think, "That's enough for today," your dog is just getting started. Coat requires only occasional brushing.

Health: A healthy bundle of energy.

Appropriate for: Beginners

QUICK INFO **FIC Group 1/No. 141:** *Sheepdogs and Cattle-dogs* **Country of Origin:** *France* **Size:** *16–18 inches (40–46 cm)* **Weight:** *17–26 pounds (8–12 kg)* **Fur:** *long and rough, very thick and slightly wavy* **Color:** *sandy to red and brown, black or gray, harlequin* **Life Expectancy:** *12 to 14 years*

Bernese Mountain Dog

History: Bred from several old Swiss farm dog breeds, it guarded the barnyard and pulled the milk wagons to the collection point. Today it is among the most beloved and beautiful farm dogs.

Training: 🐾🐾
City: no
Family: 🐾
Care: 🐾🐾🐾
Activity Level: 🐾🐾

Character: Good-natured, not particularly accommodating to strangers, loving and reliable with children, alert, and quick to learn. The Bernese Mountain dog has no inclination to wander and rarely hunts.

Living Conditions: It loves being outdoors, gladly takes long walks, but is not a runner. Can't stand the heat. Basic training (all it needs) should start early and be consistent but without force.

Health: HD, PRA, OCD, elbow dysplasia; overexertion during youth must be avoided.

Appropriate for: Beginners

QUICK INFO FIC Group 2/No. 45: *Pinschers and Schnauzers, Molossians, Swiss Mountain Dogs* **Country of Origin:** *Switzerland* **Size:** *males 25–28 inches (64–70 cm), females 23–26 inches (58–66 cm)* **Weight:** *males 79–106 pounds (36–48 kg), females 75–90 pounds (34–41 kg)* **Fur:** *long, thick, shiny* **Color:** *deep black with reddish-brown blaze and white markings on head, chest, and paws* **Life Expectancy:** *8 to 12 years*

Bichon Frisé

History: Like the many other Bichons, this dog belongs among the French miniatures; there is no agreement about their origin, and it is difficult for lay people to distinguish between them. As early as the Middle Ages these dogs appeared in paintings of noble ladies. For centuries they served nobles as living bed warmers. In the 1970s this breed suddenly surfaced again and has since become better known.

Training: 🐾
City: 🐾
Family: 🐾 🐾
Care: 🐾 🐾 🐾 🐾 🐾
Activity Level: 🐾 🐾 🐾 🐾

Character: A charming, loving, happy, playful dog. It is alert, but doesn't bark much. It prefers to give small children a wide berth. Otherwise it is very adaptable and charming.

Living Conditions: An ideal indoor dog that also likes to go for walks. Its coat care is time-consuming.

Health: Kneecap dislocation, eye problems, occasional epilepsy, and dental problems.

Appropriate for: Beginners

QUICK INFO FIC Group 9/No. 215: *Companion and Toy Dogs* **Country of Origin:** *France, Belgium* **Size:** *maximum of 12 inches (30 cm)* **Weight:** *6–13 pounds (3–6 kg)* **Fur:** *soft, thick undercoat and thicker, slightly curly topcoat* **Color:** *pure white* **Life Expectancy:** *up to 17 years*

Black Terrier

Also: *Tchiorny Terrier*

History: In the 1930s, in the kennels of the Russian army, Giant Schnauzers, Rottweilers, Airedale Terriers, and domestic Terrier-type dogs were crossed in an effort to breed the ideal duty dog. This produced an outstanding dog, but it developed such a strong bonding with its reference person that it was unsuited for the intended duty involving a variety of handlers.

Character: This dog is quick to learn, easy to train, well balanced, and tractable. A dog with good nerves is a good protector, but not overly severe.

Living Conditions: This dog becomes a well-balanced family dog with gentle, consistent training and athletic activity such as competitive dog sports and agility.

Health: HD.

Appropriate for: Beginners

Training: 🐾
City: 🐾 🐾 🐾 🐾
Family: 🐾 🐾
Care: 🐾 🐾 🐾
Activity Level: 🐾 🐾 🐾 🐾

QUICK INFO **FIC Group 2/No. 327:** *Pinschers and Schnauzers, Molossians, and Swiss Mountain and Cattledogs* **Country of Origin:** *Russia* **Size:** *25–20 inches (63–75 cm)* **Weight:** *88–143 pounds (40–65 kg)* **Fur:** *rough, thick, wavy with undercoat; easy to scissor to shape* **Color:** *black or black with gray hairs* **Life Expectancy:** *approximately 10 years*

Bloodhound

Also: *Chien de Saint-Hubert*

Training: 🐾🐾🐾🐾
City: no
Family: 🐾🐾
Care: 🐾🐾
Activity Level: 🐾🐾🐾🐾

History: Presumably a breed over seven hundred years old, it has the greatest sense of smell imaginable. It can follow trails that are several days old, but not many people use it for that purpose anymore. The name signifies that the dog has noble blood. A rare but very lively "dog monument" from a long-ago time.

Character: Universally good natured and sensible, with a wonderful, deep voice. Its gentleness runs neck and neck with its strong will, however, so it needs a resolute but kind master.

Living Conditions: It should live in the country, but under strict control; otherwise it will be off searching through woods and fields. You just have to like this dog.

Health: Cartilage defects, HD, entropion, ectropion, skin inflammations in creases, malocclusion.

Appropriate for: Specialists in tracking

QUICK INFO FIC Group 6/No. 84: *Running and Hunting Dogs* **Country of Origin:** *Belgium* **Size:** *23–27 inches (58–68 cm)* **Weight:** *88–106 pounds (40–48 kg)* **Fur:** *short and hard* **Color:** *rust brown or black and rust brown* **Life Expectancy:** *10 to 12 years*

Bolognese

History: A Bichon from Italy that existed in a similar form in antiquity. Its name comes from the northern Italian city of Bologna, and the first descriptions date from the thirteenth century. This was the favorite dog of the nobility of the de Medici family. And even such illustrious people as the Russian Czaress Katherine the Great, the Empress Maria Theresia, and Madame Pompadour enjoyed the effervescent "powder puff." These dogs make people happy just by their nature.

Training: 🐾
City: 🐾
Family: 🐾
Care: 🐾 🐾 🐾
Activity Level: 🐾 🐾

Character: Happy, lively dogs equipped with wit and intelligence. They are good watchdogs, but they don't bark constantly, and they are very adaptable.

Living Conditions: They have no overriding need for exercise, but they like to take fairly long walks. There's no likelihood of their taking off after wild animals.

Health: Luxating patella, epilepsy, dental problems.

Appropriate for: Beginners

QUICK INFO FIC Group 9 /No. 196: *Companion and Toy Dogs* **Country of Origin:** *Italy* **Size:** *10–12 inches (25–30 cm)* **Weight:** *5.5–8.8 pounds (2.5–4 kg)* **Fur:** *long, soft, curly* **Color:** *pure white* **Life Expectancy:** *over 10 years*

Bordeaux Mastiff

Also: *Dogue de Bordeaux*

History: This dog's closest ancestors must have been English Mastiffs and Bulldogs. They were used as hunting dogs for bears and jaguars, and they were occasionally misused as fighting dogs.

Training: 🐾 🐾 🐾
City: 🐾 🐾 🐾
Family: 🐾
Care: 🐾
Activity Level: 🐾 🐾 🐾

Character: Today's Bordeaux Mastiff is good-natured and well balanced, and likes to cuddle. This is a friendly family dog and it gets along well with children. As a good watchdog and protector it attacks only in the face of a serious threat. If trained properly, it has no tendency to run after wild animals.

Living Conditions: As long as it is raised without senseless harshness, it is an obedient dog. It is an interesting housedog if it gets plenty of exercise in an appropriate house and yard.

Health: HD, cartilage defects while growing, ectropion.

Appropriate for: Experienced owners

QUICK INFO FIC Group 2/No. 116: *Pinschers and Schnauzers, Molossians, Swiss Mountain Dogs* **Country of Origin:** *France* **Size:** *males 24–27 inches (60–68 cm), females 23–26 inches (58–66 cm)* **Weight:** *110–143 pounds (50–65 kg)* **Fur:** *short, fine, soft* **Color:** *reddish brown with brown or black mask* **Life Expectancy:** *around 10 years*

Border Collie

History: This dog is at home in the borderlands between England and Scotland. One typical trait is its crouching posture as it herds sheep. This highly intelligent bundle of energy can control the flock all by itself.

Training: 🐾
City: no
Family: 🐾 🐾 🐾
Care: 🐾 🐾
Activity Level: 🐾 🐾 🐾 🐾 🐾

Character: Obedient, manageable, endearing, and easy to control. Its herding behavior and tremendous drive are instinctive.

Living Conditions: When put to work in its natural capacity as a herd dog, its mental and physical exercise needs are satisfied. When it is adequately trained and used in agility trials or fly-ball contests, its ambition and intelligence are challenged and its needs will also be adequately fulfilled.

Health: Retinal atrophy (PRA), HD, epilepsy, deafness.

Appropriate for: Experienced owners

QUICK INFO FIC Group 1/No. 297: *Sheepdogs and Cattle-dogs* **Country of Origin:** *Great Britain* **Size:** *20–21 inches (51–53 cm)* **Weight:** *29–44 pounds (13–22 kg)* **Fur:** *waterproof, double, medium length* **Color:** *normally black and white; also many colors, but white should not predominate* **Life Expectancy:** *10 to 14 years and over*

Border Terrier

History: The Border Terrier originated in the English county of Cumberland, on the border with Scotland. It was bred as a pure hunting terrier to drive a fox pursued by a pack from its den. It had good endurance and speed to keep up with a pack of hounds.

Training: 🐾 🐾
City: 🐾 🐾 🐾 🐾
Family: 🐾
Care: 🐾 🐾
Activity Level: 🐾 🐾 🐾 🐾 🐾

Character: This varmint-hunting, typical Terrier fears no adversary even today. It is clever and exceptionally trainable. It gets along well with children as long as they respect it. It loves exercise and sports. It is generally friendly toward other dogs.

Living Conditions: A poorly trained Border can be a nuisance. It needs to be kept busy because it likes to hunt. In an agility course, when a Terrier races over the obstacles, there isn't a dry eye among its opponents in the event.

Health: Rare heart problems, HD, PRA, cataracts, cryptorchidism.

Appropriate for: Beginners

QUICK INFO FIC Group 3/No. 10: *Terriers* **Country of Origin:** *Great Britain* **Size:** *approximately 13 inches (33 cm)* **Weight:** *11–16 pounds (5.1–7.1 kg)* **Fur:** *hard with tight, thick undercoat* **Color:** *red, wheat colors, gray streaked, tans, blue* **Life Expectancy:** *up to 15 years*

Borzoi

Also: *Russian Wolfhound*

History: Presumably Borzoi-type dogs were bred long ago by the Tartars. In the fourteenth and fifteenth centuries large packs were used for hunting wolves and other game.

Training: 🐾 🐾 🐾 🐾
City: no
Family: 🐾 🐾 🐾
Care: 🐾 🐾
Activity Level: 🐾 🐾 🐾 🐾 🐾

Character: Proud composure and reserved nature with strangers. This elegant dog needs close contact with people, and it is very pleasing and gentle with them. It can be trained with consistency and patience but, like all Sighthounds, without force.

Living Conditions: Since the Borzoi hunts mercilessly when allowed to run free, controlled training is very time consuming. These dogs tend to vegetate without adequate exercise.

Health: No common illnesses aside from gastric torsion, usually between the ages of two and six, and metabolic bone diseases.

Appropriate for: Experienced owners

QUICK INFO FIC Group 10/No. 193: *Sighthounds*
  Country of Origin: *Russia* **Size:** *males 27–32 inches (70–82 cm), females 26–30 inches (66–77 cm)* **Weight:** *77–105 pounds (35–48 kg)* **Fur:** *straight or wavy* **Color:** *white, gold, black, cloudy, gray, striped, flecked on a white background* **Life Expectancy:** *10 to 12 years*

Boston Terrier

History: The Boston Terrier originated in the Boston area in the middle of the nineteenth century, when various fighting breeds were crossed to produce what was originally a fighting breed. Today it has long been a well-mannered family dog.

Training: 🐾 🐾
City: 🐾
Family: 🐾
Care: 🐾
Activity Level: 🐾 🐾 🐾 🐾 🐾

Character: Today's Boston Terrier is a jolly, harmless, friendly companion dog that gets along fine with children. It is alert, but doesn't bark too much. It has boundless energy for play. Since it is quite intelligent, it quickly learns all kinds of tricks.

Living Conditions: It must be trained knowledgeably, because it is a self-assured dog. It needs to be close to people, doesn't shed, and doesn't smell doggy.

Health: Cataracts, pituitary tumors, luxating patellas, anasarca, hydrocephalus, Cushing's syndrome, heart defects.

Appropriate for: Beginners

QUICK INFO **FIC Group 9/No. 140:** *Companion and Toy Dogs* **Country of Origin:** *United States* **Size:** *14–16.5 inches (36–42 cm)* **Weight:** *14–25 pounds (6.5–11.3 kg)* **Fur:** *short, smooth, and shiny* **Color:** *streaked, black or seal, with white markings* **Life Expectancy:** *12 to 15 years*

Bouvier des Flandres

History: Just like the Rottweiler in Germany (see page 189), the Bouvier in Flanders was a helper in herding cattle, kept thieves away, and pulled wagons and even canal boats. It lived under the toughest conditions, and that had a positive effect on its character today.

Training: 🐾 🐾
City: no
Family: 🐾 🐾
Care: 🐾 🐾 🐾
Activity Level: 🐾 🐾 🐾 🐾 🐾

Character: Its bear-like appearance is deceptive. It is extremely nimble and quick, athletic, and animated, and has a pronounced defensive instinct. It announces its presence only when necessary. It is sensible, and it remembers injustices and unkindness for a long time. Among its family it is restless but happy.

Living Conditions: This dog belongs to the well-known work and duty breeds and must be trained with gentle consistency. It needs lots of room and activity. It will go through fire for its family.

Health: HD, gastric torsion, lymphosarcoma, ectropion, entropion, elbow dysplasia.

Appropriate for: Experienced owners

QUICK INFO FIC Group 1/No. 191: *Sheepdogs and Cattle-dogs* **Country of Origin:** *France/Belgium* **Size:** *males 24–27 inches (62–68 cm), females 23–26 inches (59–65 cm)* **Weight:** *males 77–88 pounds (35–40 kg), females 59–77 pounds (27–35 kg)* **Fur:** *shaggy* **Color:** *dun or gray, streaked or sooty, black* **Life Expectancy:** *around 12 years*

Brandlbracke

Also: *Austrian Brandlbracke*

History: This breed belongs to the smooth-haired Austrian Brackes, which are also known as four-eyes because of the yellow spots on their eyebrows. Our ancestors thought that such four-eyed dogs would keep evil spirits away. In comparison with old depictions and descriptions from the fourteenth century, this breed has scarcely changed since then.

Training: 🐾🐾
City: no
Family: 🐾
Care: 🐾
Activity Level: 🐾🐾🐾🐾🐾

Character: An outstanding hunting dog with plenty of endurance for mountain hunting, where physical nimbleness in steep terrain and good jumping and climbing skills are important. A vocal dog on the trail and a good tracker that likes to go after wild animals and varmints. It gets around in the water as well as on land.

Living Conditions: Hunters are the best owners for this dog.

Health: No known frequent illnesses.

Appropriate for: Devoted hunters

QUICK INFO **FIC Group 6/No. 63:** *Scent Hounds and Related Breeds* **Country of Origin:** *Austria* **Size:** *19–21 inches (48–54 cm)* **Weight:** *44–48 pounds (20–22 kg)* **Fur:** *smooth, close, and short* **Color:** *black with light brown blaze, reddish brown* **Life Expectancy:** *up to 12 years*

Brittany Spaniel (Brittany)

Also: *Brittany Pointer, Epagneul Breton*

History: The Brittany Spaniel is the product of crossing the Laverack Setter (see English Setter, page 98) with medieval bird dogs. It has an outstanding nose and points solidly. This is a classic pointer and a reliable retriever that also loves the water.

Character: The small, handy pointer is very tractable, gentle, and also often sensitive. Very talented.

Living Conditions: It fits in with the family and children exceptionally well, and makes a lovely but energetic family dog. This is no couch potato, but rather a dog for outdoor life and for activities involving lots of exercise.

Health: Occasional HD, luxating patellas, epilepsy.

Appropriate for: Active families who hunt on weekends

Training: 🐾
City: 🐾 🐾 🐾 🐾 🐾
Family: 🐾
Care: 🐾 🐾
Activity Level: 🐾 🐾 🐾 🐾 🐾

QUICK INFO FIC Group 7/No. 95: Pointers **Country of Origin:** *France* **Size:** *males 19–20 inches (48–50 cm), females 18.5–19 inches (47–49 cm)* **Weight:** *approximately 44 pounds (20 kg)* **Fur:** *thick, straight or wavy, fine, but neither stiff nor silky* **Color:** *white and orange, black and white, brown and white, tricolor* **Life Expectancy:** *12 to 14 years*

Brussels Griffon

Also: *Belgian Griffon, Griffon bruxellois*

Training: 🐾🐾
City: 🐾
Family: 🐾
Care: 🐾🐾
Activity Level: 🐾🐾

History: The Brussels Griffon and the German Affenpinscher (see page 28) surely came from the same shaggy ancestors. They simply were bred in two different colors, the Affenpinscher in black and the Brussels Griffon in fox red. The Brussels Griffon is not particularly common, for it is quite difficult to breed, and its appearance may not match today's tastes.

Character: Lively, devoted, and robust, a manageable indoor dog that still likes to run and play.

Living Conditions: It doesn't bark often, and then only rather quietly, presumably because it's hard to take in air through its upturned nose. Its eyes also water a lot.

Health: Hydrocephalus, shoulder luxation, sonorous breathing.

Appropriate for: Beginners

QUICK INFO FIC Group 9/No. 80: *Companion and Toy Dogs* **Country of Origin:** *Belgium* **Size:** *10 inches (25 cm)* **Weight:** *approximately 8.8 pounds (4 kg)* **Fur:** *coarse* **Color:** *fox red* **Life Expectancy:** *15 years and longer*

Buhund

Also: *Norwegian Buhund, Norsk Buhund, Norwegian Sheepdog*

History: This dog's original duty was to guard the house and help with herding the cattle. That is expressed in the Norwegian word *bu* (dwelling or cattle) in its name. The fairly small Spitz-type dog showed its mettle in hunting bears and wolves. In Norway the breed is supported as a cultural heritage. In other places this handsome dog is practically unknown.

Character: Lively, easily trained, and friendly. It is devoted and loves children.

Living Conditions: This is a good watchdog with plenty of energy, and it likes to bark. It needs activity and exercise, and it has lots of endurance. Its owners should be knowledgeable about dogs.

Health: No diseases specific to this breed.

Appropriate for: Experienced owners

Training:	🐾🐾
City:	no
Family:	🐾
Care:	🐾
Activity Level:	🐾🐾🐾🐾🐾

QUICK INFO FIC Group 5/No. 237: *Spitzes and Primitive Dogs* **Country of Origin:** *Norway* **Size:** *16–18.5 inches (41–47 cm)* **Weight:** *40 lbs (18 kg)* **Fur:** *double-coated, thick, and tough* **Color:** *dun (like the Fjord horse) to red-yellow, dark mask is acceptable, all black, also with white collar, chest, and paws* **Life Expectancy:** *around 12 years*

Bull Mastiff

History: In the second half of the nineteenth century, English hunting wardens for property owners used crosses between Mastiffs and Bull-dogs, the Bull Mastiffs, in combating poachers. At the same time these dogs guarded the property and put a stop to the activities of game thieves.

Training: 🐾 🐾 🐾
City: 🐾 🐾 🐾 🐾 🐾
Family: 🐾
Care: 🐾
Activity Level: 🐾 🐾 🐾

Character: This dog is even-tempered, friendly with its family, and patient with children. It is indifferent to strangers. It has no tendency to roam or hunt.

Living Conditions: Just like the Bordeaux Mastiff (see page 61), to which it is almost identical, it is not a particularly enthusiastic runner, but it likes to go on walks. With kindness and consistency it is very trainable. Its defense instinct should not be aroused through play.

Health: HD, gastric torsion, cancer, entropion, PRA, elbow dysplasia.

Appropriate for: Experienced owners

QUICK INFO **FIC Group 2/No. 157:** *Pinschers and Schnauzers, Molossians, Swiss Mountain Dogs* **Country of Origin:** *Great Britain* **Size:** *24–27 inches (61–68.5 cm)* **Weight:** *88–110 pounds (40–50 kg)* **Fur:** *short, hard, smooth* **Color:** *red, fawn, streaked, dark mask* **Life Expectancy:** *approximately 10 years*

Bull Terrier

Also: *Pit Bull*

History: Around 1860 an Englishman named Hinks crossed Bulldogs and white English Terriers to create today's Bull Terrier. The goal was a light, agile dog for fighting, for at that time dog fights involved lots of money.

Character: Today this dog is basically friendly but can be aggressive. It is strong-willed and has a mind of its own. It is not always tolerant of strangers.

Living Conditions: This dog needs early socializing and continual leadership training.

Health: Tendency toward umbilical hernia, deafness, epilepsy, and in white dogs entropion, tendency toward tumors, heart and circulatory diseases, and HD.

Appropriate for: Experienced owners

Training: 🐾 🐾 🐾
City: 🐾 🐾 🐾 🐾 🐾
Family: 🐾 🐾 🐾
Care: 🐾
Activity Level: 🐾 🐾 🐾

QUICK INFO FIC Group 3/No. 11: *Terriers* **Country of Origin:** *England* **Size:** *approximately 22 inches (55 cm)* **Weight:** *around 66 pounds (30 kg)* **Fur:** *hard, short, thin, shiny* **Color:** *all except blue and liver* **Life Expectancy:** *around 10 years*

Cairn Terrier

History: Its name comes from the Gaelic word for stone: *cairn*. In Scotland, foxes, badgers, and otters hid among the many boulders. In order to hunt them, people needed an intelligent, tough dog like the Cairn Terrier.

Training: 🐾🐾
City: 🐾
Family: 🐾
Care: 🐾🐾🐾
Activity Level: 🐾🐾🐾🐾

Character: Over the years this dog has become a cute companion dog. This largely independent but not excessively stubborn dog is a happy daredevil that learns quickly, but it needs a patient owner. It is alert, but doesn't bark too much.

Living Conditions: This dog loves adventure and doesn't always want to stick to familiar paths while on a walk. It expects lots of attention and likes to tackle tasks that require cleverness. It appreciates children, mainly because they move.

Health: Glaucoma, entropion, inguinal hernia, craniomandibular osteopathy, von Willebrand's disease.

Appropriate for: Beginners

QUICK INFO FIC Group 3/No. 4: Terriers **Country of Origin:** *Great Britain* **Size:** *12 inches (30 cm)* **Weight:** *13 pounds (6 kg)* **Fur:** *harsh and water resistant with thick undercoat, needs minor trimming* **Color:** *red, cream, wheat, gray or nearly black, streaked* **Life Expectancy:** *up to 15 years*

Canaan Dog

History: This dog came from the land of Canaan in today's Israel. In the middle of the last century the Menzels began a breed using wild pariah dogs, since the imported working dogs couldn't tolerate the climate and were too susceptible to diseases.

Training: 🐾
City: 🐾 🐾 🐾 🐾
Family: 🐾 🐾 🐾
Care: 🐾
Activity Level: 🐾 🐾 🐾 🐾 🐾

Character: This medium-size dog is trainable and a good watchdog; in its modern form it is suitable only for advanced dog owners. It needs early socializing and consistent training.
Living Conditions: This dog defends its familiar grounds very aggressively. Its behavior in a strange environment is more neutral. It reacts aggressively to other dogs. Even the puppies have to be split up early, since they fight among themselves.
Health: Epilepsy, PRA, HD, thyroid diseases.
Appropriate for: Experienced owners

QUICK INFO **FIC Group 5/No. 273:** *Spitzes and Primitive dogs* **Country of Origin:** *Israel* **Size:** *20–24 inches (50–60 cm)* **Weight:** *40–55 pounds (18–25 kg)* **Fur:** *medium long, straight, harsh* **Color:** *all except gray, striped, black and tan, and tricolor* **Life Expectancy:** *14 to 15 years and longer*

Caucasian Ovtcharka

Also: *Kavkazskaia Ovtcharka*

History: Like all herd defenders, this dog is accustomed to watching over its flock and protecting it all by itself. As a defense against wolves, while it is working it wears a wide collar with projecting spikes; its ears are cropped back to the base.

Training: 🐾 🐾 🐾 🐾 🐾
City: no
Family: 🐾 🐾 🐾
Care: 🐾 🐾 🐾
Activity Level: 🐾 🐾 🐾

Character: Its pronounced self-confidence makes it partially independent of humans, and its independent behavior often can be dangerous for strangers. Within its own family, it is calm and undemanding. It resits oral commands.

Living Conditions: This dog prefers to be outdoors. It needs plenty of room and peace; otherwise it's always on guard. The yard must be very secure. This dog needs an experienced and resolute trainer.

Health: HD, ectropion, entropion.

Appropriate for: Advanced specialists

QUICK INFO **FIC Group 2/No. 328:** *Pinschers and Schnauzers, Molossians, Swiss Mountain Dogs* **Country of Origin:** *Russia* **Size:** *24–26 inches (62–65 cm)* **Weight:** *approximately 99–110 pounds (45–50 kg)* **Fur:** *long, thick with undercoat; also shorthaired* **Color:** *white, earthy, speckled or mottled* **Life Expectancy:** *approximately 10 years*

Cavalier King Charles Spaniel

History: This breed is pictured in old paintings, usually with noble ladies. These were the favorite dogs of the English kings, which is attested to by their name. In appearance this breed approaches the King Charles Spaniel (see page 140), but it has a longer snout and is somewhat larger.

Training: 🐾
City: 🐾
Family: 🐾
Care: 🐾 🐾 🐾
Activity Level: 🐾 🐾 🐾

Character: A friendly, happy, playful, loving, and very person-oriented dog. It also likes to play with children. Easy to train. Gets along with other dogs.

Living Conditions: Likes extended walks, but is content with less if the weather is not favorable.

Health: Patellar luxation, cataracts, diabetes.

Appropriate for: Beginners

QUICK INFO FIC Group 9/No. 136: *Companion and Toy Dogs* **Country of Origin:** *Great Britain* **Size:** *10–13.5 inches (25–43 cm)* **Weight:** *10–19.5 pounds (4.4–8.8 kg)* **Fur:** *soft, silky, long, with rich waves* **Color:** *black with tan markings, chestnut brown tricolor, white with chestnut brown or yellowish red blotches* **Life Expectancy:** *up to 13 years and more*

Chart Polski

Also: *Polish Greyhound*

History: Probably originated as a cross involving Polish hunting dogs, Asian Greyhounds, and the Greyhound. Polish nobles hunted on horseback with this special greyhound. Only a few specimens survived the Second World War, and they were used to rebuild the breed.

Training: 🐾 🐾
City: no
Family: 🐾 🐾
Care: 🐾
Activity Level: 🐾 🐾 🐾 🐾 🐾

Character: Very obedient. It learns easily and willingly. Close bonding with its reference person. As a housedog it is calm, friendly, and loving. Alert, but without being aggressive. Patient with children.

Living Conditions: It prefers to be kept as the solitary pet in a household. It needs lots of exercise, such as jogging and cycling with its humans.

Health: Robust and not delicate; nothing known about common diseases.

Appropriate for: Experienced owners

QUICK INFO FIC Group 10/No. 333: *Sighthounds* **Country of Origin:** *Poland* **Size:** *males 27.5–31.5 inches (70–80 cm), females 27–29.5 inches (68–75 cm)* **Weight:** *55–66 pounds (25–30 kg)* **Fur:** *short, smooth, close* **Color:** *all colors except streaked* **Life Expectancy:** *10 to 12 years*

Chesapeake Bay Retriever

History: A hunting dog that probably is a cross of Newfoundland, American hunting dogs, Water Spaniels, and Curly-coated Retrievers. It attains its highest performance in hunting ducks in cold water. Its main talent is searching about and retrieving. Its greasy, waterproof fur is good protection against the wet.

Training: 🐾
City: 🐾 🐾 🐾 🐾 🐾
Family: 🐾 🐾
Care: 🐾 🐾
Activity Level: 🐾 🐾 🐾 🐾 🐾

Character: Calm, animated, and lively. Loving and faithful to its owner. Often a one-person companion.

Living Conditions: Even though this dog forms a close bond with people, it doesn't always want to be indoors. It is a good guard dog. It needs early and ample socialization and consistent and gentle training.

Health: PRA, HD, entropion.

Appropriate for: Experienced owners

QUICK INFO FIC Group 8/No. 263: *Retrievers, Flushing Dogs, Water Dogs* **Country of Origin:** *United States* **Size:** *21–26 inches (53–66 cm)* **Weight:** *55–80 pounds (25–36.5 kg)* **Fur:** *short, water resistant, slightly greasy* **Color:** *all shades of brown, like "dead grass"* **Life Expectancy:** *10 to 12 years*

Chihuahua

History: This is the smallest dog in the world; evidently it existed as early as the Inca Empire, but only the shorthaired version. The longhaired variety was bred by American breeders, and that dog has a striking appearance.

Training: 🐾
City: 🐾
Family: 🐾 🐾 🐾
Care: 🐾
Activity Level: 🐾 🐾

Character: With good breeding, this dog is confident and full of personality. Intelligent and alert. Loving and cuddly. In encounters with large dogs it often bluffs its way through without getting hurt.

Living Conditions: It doesn't like cold and wet. In bad weather it prefers to stay home. It must be socialized early and get to know other dogs; otherwise it can turn into a barker and ignore all rules for dogs. Small, boisterous children make the dogs nervous.

Health: Occasional cleft palate, corneal edema, hydrocephalus (water on the brain), keratitis sicca, hypoglycemia.

Appropriate for: Beginners

QUICK INFO FIC Group 9/No. 218: *Companion and Toy Dogs* **Country of Origin:** *Mexico* **Size:** *5 inches (13 cm)* **Weight:** *1.1–5.5 pounds (0.5–2.5 kg)* **Fur:** *shorthair: smooth, thick, close, shiny; longhair: soft, wispy* **Color:** *all colors* **Life Expectancy:** *up to 20 years*

Chinese Crested Dog

History: Known as early as the thir-teenth century in China, this dog came to Europe only in 1960. In this breed hairy (powder puff) Crested Dogs have to be crossed again and again to produce hairless specimens.

Training: 🐾
City: 🐾
Family: 🐾 🐾
Care: 🐾 🐾 🐾
Activity Level: 🐾 🐾 🐾

Character: These are lovable, gentle, lively, and ideal indoor dogs that are appropriate even for people with allergies. They are shy with strangers. They get along well with other dogs and animals.

Living Conditions: This dog is not as sensitive to cold as peo-ple say. It is quite robust with reasonable exercise in the out-doors. In extreme cold, of course, it prefers to be indoors.

Health: Bite abnormalities, various skin allergies, sunburn.

Appropriate for: Beginners

QUICK INFO **FIC Group 9/No. 288:** *Companion and Toy Dogs* **Country of Origin:** *China* **Size:** *males 11–13 inches (28–33 cm), females 9–12 inches (23–30 cm)* **Weight:** *up to 12 pounds (5.5 kg)* **Fur:** *Hairless: soft, long tufts of hair on head, paws, and tail; Powder Puff: soft, long, and thick* **Color:** *all colors* **Life Expectancy:** *over 15 years*

Chow Chow

History: This spitz-type dog may date
to 150 B.C. and came to England in
the early 1880s from China where it
was extensively bred as long ago as
the seventh century. It was first a sled
dog. Its name was coined by English
traders and means bric-a-brac.

Training: 🐾 🐾 🐾 🐾
City: 🐾 🐾 🐾
Family: 🐾 🐾 🐾 🐾
Care: 🐾 🐾 🐾 🐾 🐾
Activity Level: 🐾 🐾 🐾

Character: It is a powerful guard dog by nature and is often
shy around strangers. It is loyal to its family, intelligent, and
trainable but arrogant and independent.

Living Conditions: It requires supervision around strangers,
gentle and consistent leadership training. It is rarely seen as a
participant in dog sports and doesn't particularly like running
but prefers solitary walks with its handler.

Health: Eczema, entropion, corneal inflammations, skin
tumors, HD, hypothyroidism, photophobia, keratitis sicca,
luxation of patella.

Appropriate for: Experienced owners

QUICK INFO **FIC Group 5/No. 205:** *Spitzes and Primitive
Dogs* **Country of Origin:** *China (Great Britain)* **Size:** *males
19–22 inches (48–56 cm), females 18–20 inches (46–51 cm)*
Weight: *55–62 pounds (25–28 kg)* **Fur:** *shorthair type rare but
on the increase; longhair version: very thick, fluffy, with soft
undercoat* **Color:** *uniform red, black, fawn, blue, and cream*
Life Expectancy: *10 to 12 years*

Clumber Spaniel

History: Originally from France. People wanted a heavy dog that was more steady, conscientious, and thorough than the nervous, light Cocker Spaniel. The Clumber was especially prized by nobles and queens.

Training: 🐾 🐾
City: 🐾 🐾 🐾
Family: 🐾 🐾 🐾 🐾
Care: 🐾 🐾 🐾 🐾
Activity Level: 🐾 🐾 🐾 🐾

Character: This dog is stoic and easygoing, somewhat slow in the hunting field but loving and dedicated to its owner. It is an expert retriever, especially in heavy cover.

Living Conditions: It makes an excellent pet in the city but has never reached popularity as a companion.

Health: HD, ectropion, undershot jaw, epilepsy. With inadequate exercise it tends toward corpulence. Careful care of ears and coat is required.

Appropriate for: Spaniel owners

QUICK INFO FIC Group 8/No. 109: *Retrievers, Flushing Dogs, and Water Dogs* **Country of Origin:** *Great Britain* **Size:** *12–14 inches (30–35 cm)* **Weight:** *55–69 pounds (25–31.5 kg)* **Fur:** *thick, straight, silky* **Color:** *white with lemon-yellow flecks* **Life Expectancy:** *up to 14 years*

Cocker Spaniel

Also: *English Cocker Spaniel*

History: Its name comes from the woodcock, which it was used for hunting in the nineteenth century. The name *spaniel* indicates that this dog may have descended from Spanish hunting dogs. They could flush game, bay on a trail, and retrieve. They were also valued for their barking on the hunt.

Character: As family dogs they are lively and playful. Friendly and receptive by nature, they are easy to train with patience and gentleness.

Living Conditions: This lively and happy dog needs lots of exercise. It enjoys agility sports and long walks in the park.

Health: Eye diseases, eczema, inflammation of outer ear canal, HD, epilepsy, Cocker rage syndrome (a nervous illness, especially in red Cockers), epidemic tremor (encephalomyelitis).

Appropriate for: Beginners

Training: 🐾 🐾
City: 🐾 🐾
Family: 🐾 🐾
Care: 🐾 🐾 🐾 🐾
Activity Level: 🐾 🐾 🐾 🐾

QUICK INFO FIC Group 8/No. 5: *Retrievers, Flushing Dogs, and Water Dogs* **Country of Origin:** *Great Britain* **Size:** *15.5–16 inches (39.5–41 cm)* **Weight:** *28–32 pounds (12.7–14.5 kg)* **Fur:** *medium long, smooth, silky; legs, chest, and ears well feathered* **Color:** *red, black, two- and three-colored* **Life Expectancy:** *12 to 15 years*

Collie (Longhair or Rough-coated)

Rough and Smooth-coated collies are bred and shown to the same standard in the United States, with the only difference being found in the coat type. The character, living conditions, and health information are identical.

Training: 🐾
City: 🐾 🐾 🐾 🐾
Family: 🐾
Care: 🐾 🐾 🐾
Activity Level: 🐾 🐾 🐾 🐾

History: The collie originated in Scotland as a herding dog, probably in the late nineteenth century. Over the years it has been bred in many different colors and combinations of colors and is seen in both the smooth and rough coat varieties.

Character: This is a proud, intelligent, and highly trainable dog that has been adopted by families the world over as a wonderful companion, fearless watchdog, and show dog competitor.

Living Conditions: This dog performs well in dog sports, obedience, and tracking, and it loves long walks with its handlers.

Health: Entropion, microphthalmia, optic nerve hypoplasia, recessive ectasia, dwarfism, corneal dystrophy, PRA, epilepsy, patent ductus arteriosus, and deafness.

Appropriate for: Beginners

QUICK INFO FIC Group 1 /No. 156: *Sheepdogs and Cattledogs* **Country of Origin:** *Great Britain* **Size:** *males 22–24 inches (56–61 cm), females 20–22 inches (51–56 cm)* **Weight:** *44–70 pounds (22–32 kg)* **Fur:** *long, straight, coarse topcoat with thick undercoat* **Color:** *sable colors with white, tricolor, or blue merle* **Life Expectancy:** *10 to 12 years*

Collie (Shorthair or Smooth-coated)

History: The smooth collie is an easier-to-care-for dog because of its short coat. It has the same origin and history as the Rough and was originally bred for the same purpose of herding and driving livestock.

Training: 🐾
City: 🐾 🐾 🐾
Family: 🐾
Care: 🐾
Activity Level: 🐾 🐾 🐾 🐾 🐾

Character: This dog is confident and proud, intelligent and hardworking, just as the long-coated variety. It too is a fine companion for adults and children alike and a respectable watchdog. This dog is gaining in popularity in dog shows.

Living Conditions: The smooth collie is an athletic performer, a willing and able sport competitor, and has equal proficiency in obedience and tracking.

Health: The two varieties share their congenital health problems. Entropion, microphthalmia, optic nerve hypoplasia, recessive ectasia, dwarfism, corneal dystrophy, PRA, epilepsy, patent ductus arteriosus, and deafness.

Appropriate for: Beginners

QUICK INFO FIC Group 1 /**No. 296:** *Sheepdogs and Cattle-dogs* **Country of Origin:** *Great Britain* **Size:** *20–24 inches (51–61 cm)* **Weight:** *40–65 pounds (18–29.5 kg)* **Fur:** *short, hard, weatherproof* **Color:** *sable-white, tricolor, blue merle* **Life Expectancy:** *10 to 12 years*

Coton de Tuléar

History: Evidently seafarers from France took this dog to Madagascar. There it was kept as a noble lapdog. Everyday citizens were forbidden under pain of fine to own such dogs. Its wool-like fur gave it its name.

Training: 🐾
City: 🐾
Family: 🐾
Care: 🐾
Activity Level: 🐾 🐾

Character: An easily trained, manageable family dog that adapts to all living conditions and is thus a good choice. Since it has a very friendly nature, it is not an exceptionally good watchdog, which makes it even more appealing.

Living Conditions: It needs no special coat care and thrives on short walks. The main thing is for it to be near its master.

Health: Very robust and not prone to illnesses.

Appropriate for: Beginners

QUICK INFO FIC Group 9 /No. 283: *Companion and Toy Dogs* **Country of Origin:** *Madagascar* **Size:** *10–11 inches (25–28 cm)* **Weight:** *12–15 pounds (5.4–6.8 kg)* **Fur:** *over three inches (8 cm) long, fine, slightly wavy* **Color:** *white, small gray or lemon yellow flecks on the ears* **Life Expectancy:** *12 to 15 years*

Curly-Coated Retriever

History: This dog's name comes from its frizzy, curly hair, which suggests its suitability as a water dog; as such it is surpassed by no other dog. It also has a protective nature, and it has been used in combating poachers. This dog is well known in New Zealand and Australia, but not in Europe.

Training: 🐾 🐾 🐾
City: no
Family: 🐾 🐾 🐾
Care: 🐾 🐾
Activity Level: 🐾 🐾 🐾 🐾 🐾

Character: It is an excellent natural retriever and is used on quail as well as waterfowl. It is trainable and is an excellent watchdog that should be kept busy.

Living Conditions: This high-energy dog will become moody and sullen if kept confined without ample exercise. It is loyal and calm when it's given sufficient challenges and retriever work. It is an excellent choice for a hunter-companion dog.

Health: Occasional HD and PRA, hypothyroidism, Cushing's syndrome.

Appropriate for: Hunters and experienced handlers

QUICK INFO FIC Group 8/No. 110: *Retrievers, Flushing Dogs, and Water Dogs* **Country of Origin:** *Great Britain* **Size:** *25–27 inches (63.5–68.5 cm)* **Weight:** *62–77 pounds (28–35 kg)* **Fur:** *small, thick, tight curls, waterproof and dirt resistant* **Color:** *black, liver* **Life Expectancy:** *10 to 15 years*

Czechoslovakian Wolfdog

History: Czech breeders have tried, as did Leendert Saarloos (see page 190), to cross a wolf with a German Shepherd to create an even better service dog. In neither case were the original expectations achieved. The inbred wolf behavior is a problem in both cases.

Training: 🐾 🐾 🐾 🐾
City: no
Family: 🐾 🐾 🐾 🐾
Care: 🐾
Activity Level: 🐾 🐾 🐾 🐾 🐾

Character: There are dogs among the Czechoslovakian wolfdogs in which the wolf behavior is very pronounced. This dog is very wary of everything new and strangers; in performance, the dog has plenty of endurance and spirit. It needs just one reference person.

Living Conditions: This dog requires secure quarters and a handler with plenty of knowledge about wolf and dog behavior. It needs lots of attention and activity.

Health: No particular known diseases.

Appropriate for: Advanced specialist owners

QUICK INFO **FIC Group 1/No. 332:** *Sheepdogs and Cattledogs* **Country of Origin:** *Slovakia* **Size:** *at least 24–25.5 inches (60–65 cm)* **Weight:** *at least 44–57 pounds (20–26 kg)* **Fur:** *wolf-type double coat with undercoat* **Color:** *yellowish, wolf gray, and silver gray* **Life Expectancy:** *10 to 12 years*

Dachshund

Also: *Dackel or Teckel*

History: This dog was originally used for hunting badgers, but its versatility also makes it a good tracker; it can follow a blood trail and find game. It is assumed that this dog was bred from mutations of short-legged Brackes. As early as 2000 B.C. the Egyptians had Dachshund-like dogs, as did the Teutons some 2000 years ago. In the Middle Ages they were referred to as badger-hounds, badger-crawlers, or den dogs. The Dachshund was bred as a pure strain beginning in 1888. There are three hair types: shorthair, wirehair, and longhair. All three breeds also come in three sizes: standard, miniature, and toy. An interesting point is that, unlike other dogs, the size is not measured at the withers, but at the chest circumference behind the front legs.

Character: An alert, robust, and devoted dog that is clever and independent. Its alleged stubbornness is its ability to make decisions without the help of its master, which in some cases, inside a badger den, for instance, could save its life. It is a good watchdog, and even sinks its teeth in if necessary. For years it has competed with the German Shepherd for the status of favorite dog in Europe.

Living Conditions: From earliest youth it must be trained and socialized lovingly but very firmly. It may not get along perfectly with small children. Buy a Dachshund only from clearly knowledgeable breeders who place the main value on the mental and physical health of their dogs.

Dachshund (continued)

Health: Dachshund paralysis, entropion, gum tumors, abnormal bite, intervertebral disc disease, diabetes, ectasia, micropthalmia, retinal hypoplasia. Striped Dachshunds are carriers of the merle gene that often is responsible for blindness and deafness.

Appropriate for: Beginners

Training: 🐾 🐾 🐾
City: 🐾
Family: 🐾 🐾
Care: 🐾
Activity Level: 🐾 🐾 🐾

QUICK INFO FIC Group 4 /No. 148: *Dachshunds* **Country of Origin:** *Germany* **Size:** *(by chest measurement) Normal, over 13.75 inches (35 cm); Dwarf Dachshund, 12–13.75 inches (30–35 cm); Toy Dachshund, up to 12 inches (30 cm)* **Weight:** *(Normal) Males, over 14.4 pounds (7 kg), females, over 14.3 pounds (6.5 kg); (Dwarf Dachshunds) males, up to 14.4 pounds (7 kg); females, under 14.3 pounds (6.5 kg); (Toy Dachshund) males, up to 8.8 pounds (4 kg); females, up to 7.7 pounds (3.5 kg)* **Fur:** *(Shorthaired Dachshund, page 89) short, tight, close, shiny; (Longhaired Dachshund, above left) soft, smooth, shiny, ample feathers on throat, ears, underbody, legs, and tail; (Wirehaired Dachshund, above right) thick, wiry, tight, with undercoat* **Color:** *Shorthaired Dachshund: black and tan, all red, reddish yellow; Longhaired Dachshund, all red, reddish yellow, black and tan; Wirehaired Dachshund, red, badger, or other dark colors* **Life Expectancy:** *12 to 14 years*

Dalmatian

History: Place and date of origin aren't specifically known, but at present the dog is thought to be from Dalmatia, a region on the Adriatic Sea north of Albania.

Training: 🐾 🐾
City: 🐾 🐾
Family: 🐾
Care: 🐾
Activity Level: 🐾 🐾 🐾 🐾 🐾

Character: A striking, pleasant companion dog that is lively and spirited. It considers two things important: closeness to its master and lots of exercise. It is watchful, but doesn't bark excessively.

Living Conditions: Hours of walking or going along with cyclists or horseback riders are the best conditions for making a Dalmatian happy.

Health: Deafness and poor vision (so in buying a puppy, get results of a hearing test), entropion, HD, allergic reactions, eczema, kidney stones, glaucoma, malocclusion.

Appropriate for: Beginners

QUICK INFO FIC Group 6/No. 153: *Scent Hounds and Related Breeds* **Country of Origin:** *Croatia* **Size:** *males 22–24 inches (55–60 cm), females 21–23 inches (54–59 cm)* **Weight:** *males 62–66 pounds (28–30 kg), females 51 pounds (23 kg)* **Fur:** *short, hard, thick, smooth, and shiny* **Color:** *pure white with evenly sized black or liver colored spots; pups are born white* **Life Expectancy:** *10 to 12 years*

Dandie Dinmont Terrier

History: This dog got its name from a character in a novel, Sir Walter Scott's "Guy Mannering." It's a relative of the Bedlington Terrier (see page 52) and belongs among the robust Scottish Terriers. It used to fight with foxes, badgers, and otters, and rarely lost. There is also a little Dandie blood in the veins of the Wirehaired Dachshund (see page 90), and that explains the combative behavior of certain individuals.

Training: 🐾 🐾
City: 🐾 🐾
Family: 🐾 🐾 🐾
Care: 🐾 🐾 🐾
Activity Level: 🐾 🐾 🐾

Character: It is pleasant to its owner, but also strong-willed. This is a one-person dog. For calm, composed people, it is a good dog for a family with children. It is wary of other dogs and animals.

Ownership: Despite its strong will, it can be trained with patience and foresight. It is still an excellent ratter and mouser.

Health: Occasional back problems, HD, Cushing's syndrome, shoulder and elbow luxation.

Appropriate for: Beginners

QUICK INFO FIC Group 3/No. 168: *Terriers* **Country of Origin:** *Great Britain* **Size:** *8–10 inches* **Weight:** *16.6 pounds (8 kg)* **Fur:** *Mixture of soft and harsh hair, about two inches (5 cm) long* **Color:** *mustard, pepper* **Life Expectancy:** *up to 13 years*

Deerhound

History: This dog accompanied the Scottish clans into the Highlands to hunt deer–hence the name. In the eighteenth century, after the English conquered the Scots, the breed had to be laboriously reconstructed.

Training: 🐾🐾🐾
City: no
Family: 🐾🐾🐾
Care: 🐾🐾
Activity Level: 🐾🐾🐾🐾🐾

Character: This was always considered the most noble of dogs. A mixture of softness and aggressiveness, this is a sensible dog in a truly rough shell. It does not impose itself, and can be very tender. It is very reserved with strangers. A Deerhound is never unpredictable.

Living Conditions: This Celtic greyhound shows its true colors in the wide-open spaces. It is an easy dog to keep as long as it has close contact with its master, lots of room, and exercise appropriate to Sighthounds.

Health: Gastric torsion, heart problems.

Appropriate for: Experienced owners

QUICK INFO FIC Group 10/No. 164: *Greyhounds*
Country of Origin: *Great Britain* **Size:** *28–32 inches (71–81 cm)*
Weight: *83.6–106 pounds (38–48 kg)* **Fur:** *hard and rough, four inches (10 cm) long* **Color:** *dark gray to sandy red, reddish dun, streaked* **Life Expectancy:** *10 to 13 years*

Doberman (Doberman pinscher)

History: In 1860 Luis Dobermann bred this reliable and intense dog from various other valiant breeds to protect him in his duties as a tax collector.

Training: 🐾🐾
City: 🐾🐾
Family: 🐾🐾🐾
Care: 🐾
Activity Level: 🐾🐾🐾🐾🐾

Character: An intense, temperamental, elegant dog with innate toughness and defensiveness. It is highly sensitive, and often also high-strung, depending on breeding. This is a typical one-person dog and almost always the mirror image of its owner.

Living Conditions: This dog is one of the duty and service breeds that belongs in gentle and consistent hands. It needs careful training without excessive force, and is not for people who are unsure of themselves.

Health: HD, heart problems, wobbler syndrome (movement and coordination disorder), deafness, hemophilia A, alopecia, elbow dysplasia.

Appropriate for: Experienced owners

QUICK INFO FIC Group 2/No. 143: *Pinschers and Schnauzers, Molossians, Swiss Mountain Dogs* **Country of Origin:** *Germany* **Size:** *males 27–28 inches (68–72 cm), females 25–27 inches (63–68 cm)* **Weight:** *66–88 pounds (30–40 kg)* **Fur:** *short, hard, and thick, close, shiny* **Color:** *black and dark brown with reddish brown markings* **Life Expectancy:** *around 10 years*

Do Khyi

Also: *Tibetan Mastiff*

History: This dog is considered the ancestor of all guardian and herding breeds and all mastiff-type dogs. A heavy, muscular, heavily furred dog with a large head and powerful jaws, which can even go up against bears.

Training:	🐾 🐾 🐾 🐾
City:	no
Family:	🐾 🐾 🐾 🐾
Care:	🐾 🐾
Activity Level:	🐾 🐾

Character: As the prototype of dogs used to protect flocks of animals, it acts independently in certain situations and is bound by no commands when it's on the defense. It is good natured (with its own family) as long as it gets early leadership and obedience training, socializing, and close contact with understanding people; still, it's not a docile housemate.

Living Conditions: Life in close quarters can lead to anxiety, stress, and nervousness that could become dangerous.

Health: HD, otherwise robust and healthy.

Appropriate for: Experienced owners

QUICK INFO FIC Group 2/No. 230: *Pinschers and Schnauzers, Molossians, and Swiss Mountain Dogs*
  Country of Origin: *Tibet* **Size:** *24–28 inches (61–71 cm)*
  Weight: *141–172 pounds (64–78 kg)* **Fur:** *thick, with thick undercoat* **Color:** *black, black and tan, golden brown, slate gray with or without tan* **Life Expectancy:** *over 10 years*

English Bulldog

Also: *Bulldog*

History: Up to the time that animal fights were banned in 1835 the Bulldog was the ideal bull biter: sturdy, short-legged, and very powerful in the neck and jaws. The lower jaw is significantly longer than the upper, and the nose is oriented toward the rear so that the dog could still breathe when it had clamped onto the bull.

Training: 🐾 🐾 🐾 🐾
City: 🐾
Family: 🐾
Care: 🐾 🐾
Activity Level: 🐾 🐾

Character: Today a friendly, devoted dog that loves its family and gets along lovingly with children. For people who insist on absolute obedience, this is not the right dog.

Living Conditions: Likes nice walks. Indoors you have to put up with its snoring. Since it doesn't take in air very well, it has a low tolerance for heat.

Health: Cleft palate, swimmer syndrome (puppies spread their legs out at right angles from the body), HD, lameness in forelegs, skin diseases, nasal contraction, among others.

Appropriate for: Beginners

QUICK INFO FIC Group 2/No. 149: *Pinschers and Schnauzers, Molossians, and Swiss Mountain Dogs* **Country of Origin:** *Great Britain* **Size:** *12–14 inches (30–35 cm)* **Weight:** *51–55 pounds (23–25 kg)* **Fur:** *short, fine, shiny* **Color:** *all colors except black and tan* **Life Expectancy:** *8 to 10 years*

English Foxhound

History: This has always been the classic pack hound of the Britons, who as early as the sixth century used it in large packs for hounding. The breed was never bred for beauty, but rather for performance, and breed standards have been observed for a very long time.

Training: 🐾 🐾 🐾 🐾
City: no
Family: 🐾 🐾 🐾 🐾 🐾
Care: 🐾
Activity Level: 🐾 🐾 🐾 🐾 🐾

Character: These dogs are lively, devoted, patient with children, affectionate, and amiable with other dogs.

Living Conditions: In spite of these qualities, these purebred hunting dogs are not generally suited for house pets, for they are happy only in a pack and living together in a kennel. Only in exceptional instances and under special conditions should individual dogs be kept in the house.

Health: Deafness, spinal osteochondrosis. Thrombocytopathy (a blood disease) occurs only in Foxhounds.

Appropriate for: Specialists (pack owners)

QUICK INFO FIC Group 6/No. 159: *Running and Scent Dogs* **Country of Origin:** *Great Britain* **Size:** *23–25 inches (58–64 cm)* **Weight:** *48–62 pounds (22–28 kg)* **Fur:** *short, thick, hard, shiny* **Color:** *all colors of Scent Hounds* **Life Expectancy:** *around 10 to 12 years*

English Setter

History: This beautiful Setter's fore-bears were Pointers and old varieties of Spaniels. Its specialties are searching, locating, and pointing. This is the fastest of the Setter breeds.

Training:	🐾🐾
City:	no
Family:	🐾🐾
Care:	🐾🐾🐾🐾🐾
Activity Level:	🐾🐾🐾🐾🐾

Character: This dog is gentle, loving, and patient with children. It gets along well with other animals. It needs lots of love and attention. It doesn't like to be left alone for very long. It doesn't accept solitary kenneling and can become obstinate. Inactivity and boredom often lead to destruction when neglected. It thrives on gentle, consistent training and plenty of regular exercise.

Living Conditions: This dog lives for hunting and running free in large fields and does poorly when its exercise needs are neglected.

Health: HD, progressive retina atrophy, hereditary deafness, skin problems; cancer is the most frequent cause of death.

Appropriate for: Experienced weekend hunters

QUICK INFO FIC Group 7/No. 2: *Pointing Dogs* **Country of Origin:** *Great Britain* **Size:** *males 25–27 inches (63–68 cm), females 24–26 inches (61–65 cm)* **Weight:** *44–66 pounds (20–30 kg)* **Fur:** *slightly wavy, long, and silky* **Color:** *white with evenly distributed yellow, orange, brown, or black spots, tricolor* **Life Expectancy:** *up to 14 years*

English Springer Spaniel

History: One of the oldest English flushing dogs, which drove birds into nets hundreds of years ago. Nowadays it is bred in working lines and purely as a show dog. An outstanding hunting dog, it searches, flushes, and ferrets out the game and retrieves nicely after the shot. Many breeds of hunting spaniels are descended from this breed.

Training: 🐾
City: 🐾 🐾 🐾
Family: 🐾
Care: 🐾 🐾 🐾
Activity Level: 🐾 🐾 🐾 🐾

Character: As an indoor dog, it is devoted, good-natured, and sincere. It is a happy playmate for the children. It loves the water and would like to spend most of the day retrieving.
Living Conditions: It needs long walks, on which its owners must keep it occupied with obedience exercises and games. It needs people with imagination.
Health: Eye problems. Regular ear care is necessary.
Appropriate for: Beginners

QUICK INFO FIC Group 8/No. 125: *Retrievers, Flushing Dogs, and Water Dogs* **Country of Origin:** *Great Britain* **Size:** *approximately 20 inches (50 cm)* **Weight:** *48–53 pounds (22–24 kg)* **Fur:** *medium long, thick, smooth, water- and weatherproof, silky, and shiny* **Color:** *black and white, brown and white, reddish-brown and white* **Life Expectancy:** *up to 15 years*

Entlebucher Cattle Dog

History: Two valleys in Luzerne, Switzerland, the Entler and the little Emme, are the narrow homeland of the Entlebucher. This dog has proven its worth on Swiss farms as a barn-yard and herding dog. By 1924 this breed was nearly extinct, but it was saved at the last minute through the efforts of Dr. Kobler, a Swiss breeder.

Training: 🐾🐾
City: 🐾🐾🐾
Family: 🐾🐾🐾
Care: 🐾
Activity Level: 🐾🐾🐾🐾🐾

Character: This dog is alert, loyal to its home, watchful, unafraid, and quick to learn. When raised with children, it watches over them patiently and dependably.

Living Conditions: This is a very active dog that wants to be kept busy. It is a good candidate for agility and dog sports, but only for people who are self-possessed. Exercise combined with tasks is extremely important for its happiness.

Health: No common diseases.

Appropriate for: Beginners

QUICK INFO FIC Group 2/No. 47: *Pinschers and Schnauzers, Molossians, and Swiss Mountain Dogs* **Country of Origin:** *Switzerland* **Size:** *16–20 inches (40–50 cm)* **Weight:** *55–66 pounds (25–30 kg)* **Fur:** *short, thick, close, hard, and shiny* **Color:** *black, with yellow to rust-brown and white markings* **Life Expectancy:** *12 to 14 years and more*

Eurasier

History: The Eurasier was intended by Julius Wipfel to be an amiable, healthy housedog. It was bred from Chow Chow, Wolfsspitz, and Samoyed stock. The breed was first named Eurasier and officially recognized in 1973.

Training: 🐾🐾🐾
City: 🐾
Family: 🐾
Care: 🐾🐾🐾
Activity Level: 🐾🐾🐾

Character: This dog has a very sociable nature. Pleasant and calm, it can still be strong willed. Very devoted and sensitive, it is a watchful companion, but not aggressive. At first it is reserved with strangers.

Living Conditions: It always wants to be part of the group, but it doesn't need much exercise. Sometimes it will fake an interest in sports, but it doesn't care much about winning. When the Eurasier runs free, sometimes the prey instinct of the Samoyed comes to the surface. With gentleness and love it is easily manageable.

Health: No common diseases.

Appropriate for: Beginners

QUICK INFO FIC Group 5/No. 291: *Spitzes and Primitive Dogs* **Country of Origin:** *Germany* **Size:** *19–24 inches (48–60 cm)* **Weight:** *40–71 pounds (18–32 kg)* **Fur:** *thick, medium-long, not tight to body, with thick undercoat* **Color:** *all colors except white, white spotted, or liver-color* **Life Expectancy:** *up to 15 years*

Field Spaniel

History: One of the few Spaniels that have been crossed with other breeds and became more stylish. Formerly it was a variety of Cocker Spaniel (see page 83). Before that it was a good hunting dog for rugged terrain. This breed was nearly extinct by 1945. Crossing Cocker and Springer Spaniels produced a nice family dog. It has a well-balanced physique.

Training: 🐾 🐾 🐾
City: 🐾 🐾 🐾 🐾
Family: 🐾 🐾
Care: 🐾
Activity Level: 🐾 🐾 🐾 🐾 🐾

Character: This is a calm, gentle dog. Since it is a little more strong willed than the other Spaniel breeds, it needs patient and consistent training.

Living Conditions: It is not as conspicuous as the other Spaniel breeds, so it is not widespread.

Health: Occasional HD. It is alleged to be sensitive to anesthetics, hypothyroidism, cleft palate, and epilepsy.

Appropriate for: Beginners

QUICK INFO FIC Group 8/No. 123: *Retrievers, Flushing, and Water Dogs* **Country of Origin:** *Great Britain* **Size:** *18 inches (46 cm)* **Weight:** *35–50 pounds (16–22.5 kg)* **Fur:** *fairly long, well feathered, thick, silky and shiny* **Color:** *all black, liver, or dappled with or without a blaze* **Life Expectancy:** *10 to 12 years*

Finnish Spitz

Also: *Suomenpystykorva*

History: This is the national dog of Finland, and it is used for hunting in the birch woods and fields in its homeland. Its ancestors probably were the Russian Laiki (see page 222). In appearance and their hunting behavior they are nearly identical.

Training: 🐾 🐾 🐾
City: no
Family: 🐾 🐾
Care: 🐾 🐾
Activity Level: 🐾 🐾 🐾 🐾 🐾

Character: This dog is independent and intelligent, and not shy. Sometimes its obedience leaves something to be desired. It is watchful but not aggressive. Its barking can sometimes be annoying. It is patient with children.

Living Conditions: It needs lots of exercise in combination with its activities. This dog is impervious to the weather and likes to be outdoors, but it also likes to be with its humans.

Health: Cleft palate, ectasia, patellar luxation, epilepsy.

Appropriate for: Experienced owners

QUICK INFO FIC Group 5/No. 49: *Spitzes and Primitive Dogs* **Country of Origin:** *Finland* **Size:** *17–20 inches (44–50 cm)* **Weight:** *approximately 44 pounds (20 kg)* **Fur:** *double coat, long, hard, topcoat with straight hairs, especially thick in the neck region, on the back, and around the trousers* **Color:** *reddish brown, yellowish brown; white markings on chest or paws are acceptable* **Life Expectancy:** *over 10 years*

Flat-Coated Retriever

History: The Flat-coated Retriever arose at the end of the nineteenth century, when many dog breeds originated or people began to breed pure strains. The breeder, named Mr. Shirley, produced this dog from Labrador Retrievers, Setters, Collies, and probably Newfoundland Retrievers. The Flat-coated was a retriever in the water and on land. Nowadays it is not used much by hunters.

Training: 🐾
City: 🐾 🐾 🐾 🐾 🐾
Family: 🐾
Care: 🐾
Activity Level: 🐾 🐾 🐾 🐾 🐾

Character: This is a tractable, devoted family dog that likes to play with children. It's easy to train and friendly with everyone, so it's not a good watch- or guard dog.

Living Conditions: This lively, lovable dog needs plenty to keep it busy and good exercise. It likes to show its intelligence. It's a surprise performer in agility and dog sports.

Health: HD, kneecap dislocation, glaucoma, epilepsy.

Appropriate for: Beginners

QUICK INFO FIC Group 8/No. 121: *Retrievers, Flushing Dogs, and Water Dogs* **Country of Origin:** *Great Britain* **Size:** *approximately 24 inches (60 cm)* **Weight:** *66–77 pounds (30–35 kg)* **Fur:** *long, smooth, thick, fine* **Color:** *black or liver* **Life Expectancy:** *approximately 10 years, but also longer*

Fox Terrier (Smooth-haired)

History: Even though the Wirehaired Fox Terrier differs from the Smooth-haired almost exclusively in the fur, they are recognized by cynologists as two different breeds. The Wirehair needs careful trimming by specialists to show its beauty, but the Smooth-haired Fox Terrier's athletic beauty is naturally evident.

Training: 🐾 🐾 🐾
City: 🐾 🐾 🐾 🐾
Family: 🐾 🐾
Care: 🐾
Activity Level: 🐾 🐾 🐾 🐾 🐾

Character: The Smooth-haired Fox Terrier is a little more tougher, adventurous, and self-assured than its wirehaired brother. Like the Wirehair, it doesn't go out of its way to avoid trouble.

Living Conditions: This dog needs either lots of hunting or even more dog sports, and once a week is far from enough. As long as it is trained and handled consistently, this is one of the gems of the dog breeds.

Health: Deafness, epilepsy, shoulder luxation, Legg-Perthes' disease, cataracts.

Appropriate for: Energetic owners

QUICK INFO **FIC Group 3/No. 12:** *Terriers* **Country of Origin:** *Great Britain* **Size:** *approximately 15 inches (39 cm)* **Weight:** *approximately 17.5 pounds (8 kg)* **Fur:** *smooth, straight, thick, short, waterproof, soft undercoat* **Color:** *white, white and tan, black and tan* **Life Expectancy:** *over 12 years*

Fox Terrier (Wirehair)

History: In both England and Scotland the fox is the shepherds' number-one enemy. They hunt these lamb thieves out of their hiding places with their lively, tough terriers and shoot them. That's the origin of this dog's name. At the start of the last century the Wirehair Fox Terrier became very fashionable as a companion dog. However, it has been spared the fate of mass breeding.

Training: 🐾 🐾 🐾
City: 🐾 🐾 🐾
Family: 🐾
Care: 🐾 🐾 🐾 🐾 🐾
Activity Level: 🐾 🐾 🐾 🐾 🐾

Character: The Wirehair is self-assured, adventurous, intelligent, and watchful.

Living Conditions: Because of its toughness and its strong prey instinct, it needs resolute early training. It is a very good candidate for dog sports. A professional is needed for regular trimming.

Health: (see Smooth-haired diseases)

Appropriate for: Active owners

QUICK INFO FIC Group 3/No. 169: *Terriers* **Country of Origin:** *Great Britain* **Size:** *15 inches (39 cm)* **Weight:** *approximately 17.5 pounds (8 kg)* **Fur:** *wiry, thick, hard, curly* **Color:** *predominantly white background color, with tan, black, or black and tan markings on head, body, and base of tail* **Life Expectancy:** *12 years and over*

French Bulldog

Also: *Bouledogue français*

History: The French Bulldog was created from English miniature bulldogs belonging to English immigrants by crossing them with Griffons and Terriers. This was initially a dog of the people rather than of the nobility.

Training:	🐾
City:	🐾
Family:	🐾
Care:	🐾
Activity Level:	🐾 🐾

Character: This dog is very tractable, affectionate, tender, always merry and undemanding. It needs close contact with people, and it likes to be the center of attention.

Living Conditions: It needs no great, long walks, but likes to be part of everything.

Health: Because of anatomical traits, natural birth is often impossible. Its short skull leads to ventilation problems and that makes this dog susceptible to heatstroke. Hemophilia A and other bleeding problems are seen, as is cleft palate and hemivertebra.

Appropriate for: Beginners

QUICK INFO **FIC Group 9 /No. 101:** *Companion and Toy Dogs* **Country of Origin:** *France* **Size:** *12 inches (30 cm)* **Weight:** *13–26.5 pounds (6–12 kg)* **Fur:** *short, soft, shiny* **Color:** *dun or fauve, streaked or white with streaky patches* **Life Expectancy:** *twelve years and over*

German Boxer (Boxer)

History: Originally a dog for hunting pigs and bears in packs, and later abused as a fighting dog, after 1860 the boxer developed over time into a manageable companion and guard dog, and it now belongs among the recognized service and work dogs.

Training: 🐾
City: 🐾🐾
Family: 🐾🐾
Care: 🐾🐾
Activity Level: 🐾🐾🐾🐾🐾

Character: It is friendly and unbelievably playful, but when necessary it is a serious defender. It has boundless patience with children. It's an easy dog to read, since you can tell its mood by its facial expression.

Living Conditions: This is an obedient dog as long as it is trained lovingly and consistently. It's a good candidate for dog sports. If idle it can cause problems.

Health: Benign or malignant tumors, hereditary spondylosis, glandular and testicular cancer, eye diseases, gastric torsion, hypothyroidism, atopy, cardiac defects.

Appropriate for: Beginners

QUICK INFO **FIC Group 2/No. 144:** *Pinschers and Schnauzers, Molossians, and Swiss Mountain Dogs* **Country of Origin:** *Germany* **Size:** *21.5–25 inches (55–63 cm)* **Weight:** *males 66–71 pounds (30–32 kg), females 53–55 pounds (24–25 kg)* **Fur:** *short, smooth, thick, shiny* **Color:** *yellow and streaked, with or without white markings* **Life Expectancy:** *8 to 9 years or more*

German Hunting Terrier

History: This dog was developed from the Fox Terrier and the Wire-haired English Terrier. The result is a versatile hunting dog that is scarcely surpassed by any other Terrier in terms of hunting enthusiasm, willingness to work, and toughness. This dog takes everything seriously. He doesn't know the meaning of charm.

Character: This dog joins together all work qualities that a hunter could desire. It's not a good companion dog because of its strong will and rough nature and its need for freedom and exercise. It is absolutely fearless and stubborn.

Living Conditions: This extremely hardworking dog breed should be kept only under absolute control. The German Hunting Terrier is rarely suited as a family dog.

Health: A robust, vital dog with no genetic problems.

Appropriate for: Hunters only

Training: 🐾 🐾 🐾 🐾
City: no
Family: no
Care: 🐾
Activity Level: 🐾 🐾 🐾 🐾 🐾

QUICK INFO **FIC Group 3/No. 103:** *Terriers* **Country of Origin:** *Germany* **Size:** *up to 16 inches (40 cm)* **Weight:** *20–22 pounds (9–10 kg)* **Fur:** *smooth or wirehair, short and hard in either case* **Color:** *black, black streaked with gray, or dark brown, also with tan markings* **Life Expectancy:** *12 to 14 years*

German Longhair

History: The German Longhair is a pointer bred according to strict specifications for high performance in hunting. Its ancestors were bird dogs and flushing dogs. It has been bred as a pure breed ever since 1879. It is especially adept at trailing, finding downed game, and working in the water.

Training:	🐾
City:	no
Family:	🐾 🐾
Care:	🐾 🐾
Activity Level:	🐾 🐾 🐾 🐾 🐾

Character: This dog has an even and calm disposition and is easily trained. It should never be aggressive toward people and other dogs because it is a field dog.

Living Conditions: It prefers a hunting home and it thrives only when used frequently in the field. It becomes bored and truculent when it is confined.

Health: A robust dog that withstands cold; it has no known hereditary diseases.

Appropriate for: Hunters

QUICK INFO FIC Group 7/No. 117: *Pointers* **Country of Origin:** *Germany* **Size:** *males 23–25 inches (63–66 cm), females 21–23 inches (60–63 cm)* **Weight:** *48–70 pounds (22–32 kg)* **Fur:** *about 1.5 inches (3.5 cm) long, close, hard with thick undercoat* **Color:** *brown with or without white markings, brown or light flecked, tri-color ticking* **Life Expectancy:** *12 to 14 years*

German Mastiff

History: The Teutons used similar dogs for hunting wild boars, though later on only the nobility had the privilege of hunting pigs with packs of dogs. Later still, they were companions for rich townspeople. Prince Bismarck even proposed the Mastiff as the national dog.

Training: 🐾 🐾
City: no
Family: 🐾
Care: 🐾
Activity Level: 🐾 🐾 🐾 🐾

Character: Good Mastiffs are gentle and good natured, loving, and calm with their humans and with children. They thrive on loving, patient training.

Living Conditions: These large dogs need room and lots of time for exercise. They want to live with the family, and they become bored and grouchy in a kennel.

Health: Check for healthy parents and siblings at purchase. Sometimes there are bone, eye, and skin diseases, and occasional deafness in striped dogs.

Appropriate for: Experienced owners

QUICK INFO FIC Group 2/No. 235: *Pinschers and Schnauzers, Molossians, Swiss Mountain Dogs* **Country of Origin:** *Germany* **Size:** *males at least 31.5 inches (80 cm), females at least 28 inches (72 cm)* **Weight:** *approximately 110 pounds (50 kg)* **Fur:** *very short, thick, shiny* **Color:** *yellow, streaked, blue, black, black and white speckled (Tiger)* **Life Expectancy:** *5 to 10 years*

German Shepherd

History: There is no other dog breed that performs so well in herding livestock, guiding blind people, helping the handicapped, rescuing people buried in avalanches, and doing police work. The German Shepherd cannot be replaced by any technical device as a helper in the army, a locater of drugs, explosives, or corpses.

Training: 🐾
City: 🐾 🐾 🐾
Family: 🐾
Care: 🐾 🐾
Activity Level: 🐾 🐾 🐾 🐾 🐾

Character: With good breeding, well socialized, and trained without force, this is a well-balanced and reliable family dog. Its watchfulness and defensive instinct are inborn.

Living Conditions: Needs daily exercise for mental as well as physical development.

Health: HD, various joint diseases, eye diseases, allergies, epilepsy, ectasia, elbow dysplasia, and dozens of others.

Appropriate for: Experienced owners

QUICK INFO FIC Group 1/No. 166: *Sheepdogs and Cattledogs* **Country of Origin:** *Germany* **Size:** *22–26 inches (55–65 cm)* **Weight:** *62–77 pounds (28–35 kg)* **Fur:** *short, weatherproof topcoat with undercoat* **Color:** *black layer with brown, yellow, or gray markings, all black or wolf gray, or with brown markings* **Life Expectancy:** *12 to 14 years*

German Shorthair

History: The German Shorthair, like the German Wirehair (see page 115), is a jack of all trades. Its elegant appearance comes from the English Pointer (see page 180). It is one of the widespread and beloved German hunting dogs, and it adapts to every climate.

Training: 🐾
City: no
Family: 🐾 🐾 🐾
Care: 🐾
Activity Level: 🐾 🐾 🐾 🐾 🐾

Character: This extremely lively and wiry working dog needs good training. It learns quickly and is easily trained. It gets along fine with children.

Living Conditions: It likes very close contact with its humans. This very lively dog is tolerable in the family if it is used for hunting or sports to burn energy. Keeping this dog exclusively as a pet works only if it has something to keep it busy all day long.

Health: HD, entropion, ear inflammations, pannus, melanoma.

Appropriate for: Knoweldgeable owners

QUICK INFO **FIC Group 7/No. 119:** *Pointers* **Country of Origin:** *Germany* **Size:** *males 23–26 inches (58–65 cm), females 21–23 inches (53–59 cm)* **Weight:** *44–70 pounds (22–32 kg)* **Fur:** *short, tight, somewhat rough* **Color:** *all brown or with white or speckled markings or blotches, light and black flecking with and without white blotches* **Life Expectancy:** *10 to 12 years*

German Wachtelhund

History: This flushing dog comes from the Brackes and is an early stage of pointer with regard to development. Also referred to as the German Spaniel in England, it is used in Germany for hunting in the woods, which shows it to be very versatile. Its strengths are flushing and finding, tracking, and searching. It is also a good water dog and a reliable retriever.

Training: 🐾🐾
City: no
Family: 🐾🐾🐾🐾
Care: 🐾🐾
Activity Level: 🐾🐾🐾🐾🐾

Character: The German Wachtelhund is a tough hunter, intense, animated, and self-assured.

Living Conditions: This dog is in its element in the hunting field, and it wants close contact with its handler. In general it also does well in a family environment if hunting is part of that environment.

Health: A robust dog with no particular genetic diseases.

Appropriate for: Hunting families

QUICK INFO FIC Group 8/No. 104: *Retrievers, Flushing Dogs, and Water Dogs* **Country of Origin:** *Germany* **Size:** *18–21 inches (45–54 cm)* **Weight:** *approximately 44 pounds (20 kg)* **Fur:** *strong, thick, wavy, tight, shiny* **Color:** *brown and speckled brown* **Life Expectancy:** *up to 15 years*

German Wirehair

History: The German Wirehair is the all-around dog among pointers. It shines in all types of hunting. Anyone who hunts with this dog needs no other canine help. Its fur protects it from rough weather and terrain.

Training: 🐾
City: no
Family: 🐾 🐾
Care: 🐾
Activity Level: 🐾 🐾 🐾 🐾 🐾

Character: This is a tough hunting dog that also has a generous amount of intelligence. It is reserved with strangers, but not aggressive. As long as the German Wirehair is kept busy, it is friendly, loving, and composed.

Living Conditions: The German Wirehair is the happiest dog when it can perform its outdoor duties. If it's not kept busy, it gets bored or anxious, it vegetates, and develops behavior problems.

Health: Generally very robust. Watch out for HD, entropion, and gastric torsion.

Appropriate for: Hunters only

QUICK INFO *FIC Group 7/No. 98: Pointers* **Country of Origin:** *Germany* **Size:** *males 24–26.5 inches (60–67 cm), females 22–24 inches (55–60 cm)* **Weight:** *62–77 pounds (28–35 kg)* **Fur:** *hard, weatherproof wirehair, double* **Color:** *brown and black or brown with white flecks* **Life Expectancy:** *up to 14 years*

115

Giant Schnauzer

History: This breed developed in the nineteenth century from butchers' and farmers' dogs. We no longer can determine just what dogs were used, but they might include the Great Dane. It is sometimes called a Russian Schnauzer, a bear Schnauzer; in Munich, Germany, it was used to guard the beer wagons, so it is also referred to as a beer Schnauzer.

Training: 🐾 🐾
City: 🐾 🐾 🐾 🐾
Family: 🐾 🐾
Care: 🐾 🐾 🐾
Activity Level: 🐾 🐾 🐾 🐾 🐾

Character: Like the standard Schnauzer, this dog can be a spirited go-getter; yet it can also be calm and sedate. It has a hereditary guarding instinct that it turns on when needed, but it can also be well mannered and gentle.

Living Conditions: This dog must be trimmed regularly, or else it will turn into a bear Schnauzer again. With appropriate direction, it can do very well in sports, but it's not considered a particularly tractable dog.

Health: HD, knee problems, OCD, von Willebrand's disease, hypothyroidism.

Appropriate for: Experienced owners

QUICK INFO **FIC Group 2/No. 81:** *Pinschers and Schnauzers, Molossians, and Swiss Mountain and Cattledogs* **Country of Origin:** *Germany* **Size:** *25.5–27.5 inches (65–70 cm)* **Weight:** *approximately 77 pounds (35 kg)* **Fur:** *wiry, hard, with soft undercoat* **Color:** *black, salt and pepper* **Life Expectancy:** *10 to 12 years*

Golden Retriever

History: The originator of the Golden Retriever was Lord Tweedmouth. In 1868 he used a yellow Labrador, a Tweed Water Spaniel, an Irish Setter, and a sand-colored Bloodhound as the starting breeds for the Goldie. In 1913 the Golden Retriever gained recognition as a breed.

Training: 🐾
City: 🐾 🐾 🐾 🐾
Family: 🐾
Care: 🐾 🐾 🐾
Activity Level: 🐾 🐾 🐾 🐾 🐾

Character: This is a great friend to children. It is easy to train and gentle, compatible with other animals in the household. This is not a one-person dog, but rather an adaptable family dog.

Living Conditions: A passionate swimmer and retriever, an outdoor dog that needs lots of exercise and activity. A good candidate for dog sports. It's great popularity has brought this breed many problems. Buy a puppy only from a recognized breeder, and choose carefully.

Health: HD, eye problems, PRA, epilepsy, cataracts, hypothyroidism, osteosarcoma.

Appropriate for: Beginners

QUICK INFO FIC Group 8 /No. 111: *Retrievers, Flushing Dogs, and Water Dogs* **Country of Origin:** *Great Britain* **Size:** *males 22–24 inches (56–61 cm), females 20–22 inches (51–56 cm)* **Weight:** *males 70–81.5 pounds (32–37 kg), females 59–70.5 pounds (27–32 kg)* **Fur:** *straight or slightly wavy topcoat with fringe and waterproof undercoat* **Color:** *all shades of gold or wheat blonde* **Life Expectancy:** *12 to 15 years*

Gordon Setter

History: The Gordon Setter, the heaviest of the Setter breeds, arose at the end of the eighteenth century in the kennel of the Duke of Gordon. It was particularly well suited for hunting in rough terrain, because it was more

Training: 🐾 🐾
City: 🐾 🐾 🐾 🐾 🐾
Family: 🐾 🐾 🐾 🐾
Care: 🐾 🐾 🐾
Activity Level: 🐾 🐾 🐾 🐾 🐾

powerful and had more endurance than the other setters. It tracked the game calmly and sedately and pointed by sitting (hence the name *Setter*) until the hunter arrived.

Character: A self-assured late developer with a tremendous hunting instinct, it also loves the water. Its strong-willed nature requires early and continued training.

Living Conditions: The Gordon Setter is a one-person dog, but with consistent training it is also a good family dog. It still needs lots of sporting activity and accompanying exercise.

Health: Rarely HD, PRA, thyroid gland disorders.

Appropriate for: Experienced owners

QUICK INFO FIC Group 7/No. 6: *Pointers* **Country of Origin:** *Great Britain* **Size:** *males 26 inches (66 cm), females 24 inches (62 cm)* **Weight:** *males 55–80 pounds (25–36 kg), females 44–68 pounds (20–31 kg)* **Fur:** *long, silky* **Color:** *deep black with chestnut blaze, small white spot on chest is acceptable* **Life Expectancy:** *over 10 years*

Gos d'Atura Catalá

Also: *Catalan Sheepdog and Perro de Pastor Catalan*

Training: 🐾
City: 🐾 🐾 🐾 🐾
Family: 🐾 🐾
Care: 🐾 🐾 🐾
Activity Level: 🐾 🐾 🐾 🐾 🐾

History: These dogs have been used for centuries for guarding herds. The breed originated in the eighteenth century. Since they were never bred for beauty, but rather for performance, even up to this day, dogs of this breed come in several types. Rarely is there a shorthaired version.

Character: Like all herding dogs, these dogs are intelligent and pleasant, watchful, and somewhat reserved with strangers. Males can be very independent.

Living Conditions: Since this dog is impervious to the weather, it is happy to spend its time outdoors, but it also likes to be with its people. It likes to run and needs athletic people who can give it lots of exercise.

Health: No common diseases.

Appropriate for: Beginners

QUICK INFO **FIC Group 1 /No. 87:** *Sheepdogs and Cattledogs* **Country of Origin:** *Spain* **Size:** *18–22 inches (45–55 cm)* **Weight:** *approximately 44 pounds (20 kg)* **Fur:** *harsh, medium-long, with undercoat* **Color:** *brown, sandy, gray and black with light markings* **Life Expectancy:** *over 10 years*

Great Japanese Dog (Akita)

Formerly: *American Akita Inu*

History: In 1937 the blind American author Helen Keller received two Akita Inus as a gift. In 1999 the FCI changed the name of the American Akita to the Great Japanese Dog. The AKC recognizes the name of this breed as Akita.

Training: 🐾 🐾 🐾
City: 🐾 🐾
Family: 🐾 🐾
Care: 🐾 🐾
Activity Level: 🐾 🐾

Character: A proud, self-assured dog that requires continued leadership training. Calm and unobtrusive in the home, it rarely barks. With early, consistent training it blends in harmoniously with the family. It tolerates children in its own family, but is reserved with strangers.

Living Conditions: It needs close bonding with its family and plenty of fresh air, but this doesn't mean aimless activity. It is known to become aggressive when kept in a kennel.

Health: KD, PRA, epilepsy, immune system disorders, HD, entropion.

Appropriate for: Experienced owners

QUICK INFO Group 2/No. 344: *Pinschers and Schnauzers, Molossians, and Swiss Mountain Dogs* **Country of Origin:** *Japan* **Size:** *males 25.5–27.5 inches (65–70 cm), females 24–25.5 inches (60–65 cm)* **Weight:** *99–110 pounds (45–50 kg)* **Fur:** *double, thick, slightly erect; with thick undercoat* **Color:** *all colors including white, streaked, and spotted* **Life Expectancy:** *10 years and longer*

Great Münsterländer

History: Its ancestors are the bird dogs of the Middle Ages, and for a long time it was considered simply a different colored German Longhair. It has been intentionally bred as a pure strain since 1919. The Great Münsterländer is a very versatile and handsome flushing dog, pointer, and retriever.

Training: 🐾
City: no
Family: 🐾
Care: 🐾 🐾
Activity Level: 🐾 🐾 🐾 🐾 🐾

Character: Often sensitive and nervous. A hardworking dog that learns quickly. If given a sufficient mental and physical challenge, it is a well-balanced, loving, tractable, and very devoted family dog. It is also very watchful and effective against vermin.

Living Conditions: This dog belongs in the family of a hunter, for it thrives on hunting activity. It also should have an opportunity to swim.

Health: Few health problems.

Appropriate for: Experienced owners

QUICK INFO **FIC Group 7/No. 118:** *Pointers* **Country of Origin:** *Germany* **Size:** *males 24 inches (61 cm), females 23 inches (59 cm)* **Weight:** *55–64 pounds (25–29 kg)* **Fur:** *long, thick, straight, short, and close on head* **Color:** *white with black splotches or mottled black, black head, possible white blaze* **Life Expectancy:** *10 years and longer*

Great Swiss Cattle Dog

History: This breed is descended from the Molossian types and is the forebear of the Saint Bernard (see page 191). In Switzerland these dogs served as farm dogs and herders for farmers and butchers, and as draft dogs for peddlers. This dog has been bred as a pure strain since 1908.

Training: 🐾
City: no
Family: 🐾
Care: 🐾
Activity Level: 🐾 🐾 🐾

Character: An imposing dog with an innate defense instinct. Somewhat reserved toward strangers until it gets to know them. Generally friendly, well adjusted, calm, with a high tolerance threshold, and easy to train. Does not tend to wander.

Living Conditions: This dog has no great need to run, but likes pleasant strolls, where it can use its outstanding nose to "read the news." In the home it needs adequate space, and the yard should also be larger. Playful tasks that engage its intelligence are good for it.

Health: HD and joint problems.

Appropriate for: Knowledgeable owners

QUICK INFO FIC Group 2/No. 58: *Pinschers and Schnauzers, Molossians, Swiss Mountain Dogs* **Country of Origin:** *Switzerland* **Size:** *males 26–28.5 inches (65–72 cm), females 23.5–27 inches (60–68 cm)* **Weight:** *approximately 88 pounds (40 kg)* **Fur:** *short, thick, shiny* **Color:** *black with brownish red blaze and white markings* **Life Expectancy:** *8–10 years or more*

Greyhound

History: This ancient breed radiates aristocratic bearing and speed. Emperors and queens have adorned themselves with these dogs. Nowadays they are primarily used for racing, although in the United States many are family pets used for showing and sight hound competition.

Training: 🐾 🐾
City: no
Family: 🐾 🐾
Care: 🐾
Activity Level: 🐾 🐾 🐾 🐾 🐾

Character: Greyhounds are loving, calm, adaptable house pets. They are friendly and unobtrusive. Retired racing dogs are usually quick to become admired pets.

Living Conditions: A large, secure yard is essential, for a Greyhound, with its very strong prey instinct, should run only on safe terrain. Exercise on a good racetrack is highly recommended.

Health: von Willebrand's disease, lens luxation, bloat.

Appropriate for: Experienced owners

QUICK INFO FIC Group 10/No. 158: *Greyhounds* **Country of Origin:** *Great Britain* **Size:** *males 30–31 inches (71–78 cm), females 27–28 inches (68.5–71 cm)* **Weight:** *55–66 pounds (25–30 kg)* **Fur:** *short, smooth, tight to body* **Color:** *all colors with or without white markings* **Life Expectancy:** *around 10 years*

Groenendael (Belgian Shepherd)

History: This is the black dog among the Belgian Shepherds; it was introduced as a pure breed by Professor Reul in 1891. These are medium-sized dogs with lots of endurance; they work independently as sheep dogs and have a guard instinct. They have developed differently in certain areas, and ever since their introduction they have been bred as a pure breed. Nicholas Rose rendered exceptional service to this breed.

Training: 🐾
City: 🐾🐾🐾
Family: 🐾
Care: 🐾🐾🐾
Activity Level: 🐾🐾🐾🐾

Character: Tractable, hardworking, reliable with children and very pleasant as a family dog. It is watchful but not aggressive. Early, consistent training is required.

Living Conditions: The Groenendael needs to be kept occupied and to have tasks that develop its intelligence. This is a good candidate for competitive dog sports and agility.

Health: HD, epilepsy.

Appropriate for: Beginners

QUICK INFO **FIC Group 1/No. 15:** *Sheepdogs and Cattledogs* **Country of Origin:** *Belgium* **Size:** *males approximately 24.5 inches (62 cm), females 23 inches (58 cm)* **Weight:** *males 59–70 pounds (27–32 kg), females 50–55 pounds (22.5–25 kg)* **Fur:** *long, smooth, double* **Color:** *black* **Life Expectancy:** *12–14 years*

Harz Fox

Also: *Harzer Fuchs*

History: This dog is a symbol of the nearly extinct old German herding dogs. Survived through state support almost exclusively in the old East Germany. Since 1989 the study group for the breeding of old German herding dogs has sought to assure the continuance of this breed. Further old German herding dogs include the Westerwalder Fuchs or Kuhhund, Galbbacke, Stumper, Strobel, Black Old German, and Tiger.

Character: Like all herding breeds, this dog is adaptable, eager to learn, family oriented, and watchful, and it has plenty of endurance.

Living Conditions: The Harz Fox is a good companion and family dog, like other herding dogs, if it gets enough exercise and can satisfy its will to work.

Health: A naturally healthy dog with a very good inbred disposition.

Appropriate for: Beginners

Training: 🐾
City: 🐾 🐾 🐾 🐾 🐾
Family: 🐾 🐾 🐾
Care: 🐾 🐾
Activity Level: 🐾 🐾 🐾 🐾 🐾

QUICK INFO **FIC Group:** *Not recognized* **Country of Origin:** *Germany* **Size:** *20–24 inches (50–60 cm)* **Weight:** *55–66 pounds (25–30 kg)* **Fur:** *double coat with undercoat* **Color:** *reddish brown* **Life Expectancy:** *12–14 years*

Havanese

Also: *Bichon havanais*

History: This dog is part of the Bichon group, and thus belongs among the oldest lapdogs; mummified dogs of this type have been found in tombs of pharaohs in Egypt. This breed is most common in the western Mediterranean region.

Training:	🐾
City:	🐾
Family:	🐾
Care:	🐾 🐾 🐾
Activity Level:	🐾 🐾 🐾

Character: What endears this dog to its owners is its puppy-like cheerfulness, which it retains into old age. The Havanese performs the most comical things just to be the center of attention. Its fur is odorless, and the dog does not shed.

Living Conditions: This is a good dog both for people who live alone and for families with children. In the summer it should have an opportunity to go swimming. Normal walks are adequate, but its passion is learning how to do tricks.

Health: Patellar luxation, epilepsy.

Appropriate for: Beginners

QUICK INFO FIC Group 9/No. 250: *Companion and Toy Dogs* **Country of Origin:** *western Mediterranean Region* **Size:** *8–11 inches (20–28 cm)* **Weight:** *13 pounds (6 kg)* **Fur:** *long, silky, slightly wavy* **Color:** *white, champagne, gray, gold, all shades of brown with or without white flecks* **Life Expectancy:** *14 to 16 years*

Hovawart

History: The Hovewart (courtyard defender) of the Middle Ages has nothing to do with the present Hovawart. In 1920 Kurt F. Konig mixed various farm, herd, and mountain dogs with Newfoundland, German Shepherds, Kuvasz, and Leonbergers. This breed gained recognition in 1937.

Training: 🐾
City: 🐾 🐾 🐾 🐾
Family: 🐾
Care: 🐾 🐾
Activity Level: 🐾 🐾 🐾 🐾

Character: A reliable watchdog and defender, it can distinguish between good and bad even without guard dog training. It loves its master and its family, but needs early, consistent, and gentle training.

Living Conditions: Important are bonding with the family, lots of fresh air, and appropriate activity. Its joy in overly ambitious competitive dogs sports and agility exercises is often overrated by many breeders.

Health: Cartilage defects during growth, knee problems.

Appropriate for: Experienced owners

QUICK INFO FIC Group 2/No. 190: *Pinschers and Schnauzers, Molossians, and Swiss Mountain Dogs* **Country of Origin:** *Germany* **Size:** *males 25–27.5 inches (63–70 cm), females 23–25.5 inches (58–65 cm)* **Weight:** *males 66–88 pounds (30–40 kg), females 55–77 pounds (25–35 kg)* **Fur:** *slightly wavy, nearly straight, long hair* **Color:** *blonde, black, and black markings* **Life Expectancy:** *10 to 12 years or more*

Irish Setter

Also: *Irish Red Setter*

History: This fine hunting dog has had ups and downs during the past 40 years and was grossly overbred in the 1970s. In its present form it is still a hunting dog but, with the help of conscientious breeders, is making the transition to family pet.

Character: As a hunting dog it needs mental and physical exercise but is a loving dog that's eager to learn.

Living Conditions: When maintained as a family pet it should be kept busy with dog sports and, if possible, weekend hunting.

Health: HD, skeletal problems, hydrocephalus (water on the brain), PRA, entropion, cataracts, OCD.

Appropriate for: Experienced owners

Training: 🐾🐾
City: no
Family: 🐾🐾
Care: 🐾🐾🐾
Activity Level: 🐾🐾🐾🐾🐾

QUICK INFO FIC Group 7/No. 120: *Pointers* **Country of Origin:** *Ireland* **Size:** *25–27 inches (63–68 cm)* **Weight:** *60–68 pounds (27–31 kg)* **Fur:** *long, silky* **Color:** *mahogany red with no black* **Life Expectancy:** *10 to 12 years*

Irish Soft-Coated Wheaten Terrier

History: Poor Irish farmers created a versatile dog that was everything wrapped up in one: a barnyard dog, a guard dog, and a hunting dog. In addition, it hunted rats and mice and partly fed itself with them.

Training: 🐾
City: 🐾 🐾 🐾
Family: 🐾
Care: 🐾 🐾 🐾
Activity Level: 🐾 🐾 🐾 🐾

Character: We have grown to know this dog only in the past few years. But we have been quick to appreciate its versatile and positive domestic qualities: devotion, trainability, and friendliness toward humans. This dog is spirited and playful, patient with children, and easy to train. If it weren't a "dirt collector" with its fur, it would be a nearly ideal dog.

Living Conditions: Because of its many abilities, as a family dog it needs lots of activity and exercise as a replacement for work. Even as a sporting dog it holds its own.

Health: PRA, cataracts, renal dysplasia, heart disease.

Appropriate for: Beginners

QUICK INFO FIC Group 3/No. 40: *Terriers* **Country of Origin:** *Ireland* **Size:** *18–19 inches (46–48 cm)* **Weight:** *35–40 pounds (15.75–18 kg)* **Fur:** *long and soft* **Color:** *every shade between light wheat and reddish gold* **Life Expectancy:** *10 to 12 years*

Irish Terrier

History: Irish farmers and hunters developed the Irish Terrier by selecting for performance under hard working conditions. Since it's too large for burrowing, it surely was used for combating various predators. It also easily killed rabbits and badgers.

Training: 🐾 🐾 🐾
City: 🐾 🐾 🐾 🐾
Family: 🐾 🐾 🐾
Care: 🐾 🐾 🐾
Activity Level: 🐾 🐾 🐾 🐾 🐾

Character: This dog fears nothing. It doesn't know the meaning of the word *fear*. Romping around with other dogs is its life's elixir. It has a strong personality that needs consistent training. This dog is intelligent and quick to learn. It is gentle and devoted to its family.

Living Conditions: This mischievous fellow requires supervised playtime. As an outlet for its hunting skills, it needs to take part in dog sports, obedience, terrier trials and other mental and physical exercises. It needs regular trimming.

Health: Kidney stones, eczema, bald spots in the coat, deformation of footpads.

Appropriate for: Experienced owners

QUICK INFO FIC Group 3/No. 139: *Terriers* **Country of Origin:** *Ireland* **Size:** *17–18 inches (46–48 cm)* **Weight:** *approximately 28 pounds (12.5 kg)* **Fur:** *hard, wiry, with soft undercoat* **Color:** *uniform red* **Life Expectancy:** *12 to 14 years*

Irish Water Spaniel

History: This dog looks more like a poodle than a spaniel. It's recognizable as a water dog only by its frizzy, waterproof fur. It has been a pure breed since 1850. While hunting, it's impervious to swampy terrain and ice-cold seawater.

Training: 🐾🐾🐾
City: no
Family: 🐾🐾🐾
Care: 🐾🐾🐾
Activity Level: 🐾🐾🐾🐾🐾

Character: It is an obedient and trainable dog that's primarily a hunting dog, but also makes a good family pet if weekend hunting is practiced and training takes place early on. It is reserved with strangers and is mainly an adult's dog.

Living Conditions: In general the Irish Water Spaniel is not very common; because of the nature of its coat it shouldn't be kept as a family dog without a chance to hunt.

Health: HD, malocclusion.

Appropriate for: Knowledgeable owners

QUICK INFO FIC Group 8/No. 124: *Retrievers, Flushing Dogs, and Water Dogs* **Country of Origin:** *Ireland* **Size:** *20–23 inches (51–58 cm)* **Weight:** *44–64 pounds (20–29 kg)* **Fur:** *thick, tight, crinkly curls on the body, throat, and four inches (10 cm) below the tail, not woolly, with natural sebum content* **Color:** *brown* **Life Expectancy:** *approximately 12 years*

Irish Wolfhound

History: The largest and strongest of all dogs was used for hunting elk and wolves; however, this Irish breed also made a strong impression as a companion dog. Bred from wolfhounds such as the deerhound, German Mastiff, and Borzoi, the breed had to be revitalized after around 1860, for it was nearly extinct.

Training: 🐾🐾
City: no
Family: 🐾🐾🐾
Care: 🐾
Activity Level: 🐾🐾🐾🐾🐾

Character: This dog is also known as the "gentle giant." It is calm in the house and even-tempered, and it loves its family, which it always wants to keep around it. It is no guard dog.

Living Conditions: This giant needs lots of room in the house and a large yard that is securely fenced. It likes long walks and thrives on dog-park exercise where it can run free.

Health: HD, bone and joint problems, heart diseases, gastric torsion, hereditary lameness in hindquarters, PRA.

Appropriate for: Experienced owners

QUICK INFO FIC Group 10/No. 160: *Sighthounds* **Country of Origin:** *Ireland* **Size:** *males at least 31 inches (79 cm), females 28 inches (71 cm)* **Weight:** *males at least 119 pounds (54 kg), females at least 89 pounds (40.5 kg)* **Fur:** *hard, rough, weatherproof* **Color:** *gray, striped, red, black, white, tan* **Life Expectancy:** *6 to 7 years*

Italian Greyhound

Also: *Piccolo Levriero Italiano*

History: Apparently these smallest greyhounds existed in their present form as early as in antiquity. They were always favorites of kings and emperors, such as Frederick the Great, Catherine the Great, and Queen Victoria. Dogs from good breeding are robust and tough hunting and racing dogs.

Character: Greyhounds are lively and love to run around outdoors. They are peaceful and never disruptive. Even though they appear so fragile, they have a strong personality and lots of spirit. They are often fairly reserved with strangers.

Living Conditions: They need close contact with their family, but are not good candidates for rough play with children. These dogs are ideal for people with no small children.

Health: Thyroid problems, tooth problems, epilepsy, kneecap dislocation.

Appropriate for: Beginners

Training: 🐾
City: 🐾
Family: 🐾 🐾
Care: 🐾
Activity Level: 🐾 🐾 🐾

QUICK INFO **FIC Group 10/No. 200:** *Sighthounds*
Country of Origin: *Italy* **Size:** *13–15 inches (32–38 cm)*
Weight: *11 pounds (5 kg)* **Fur:** *very short and fine* **Color:**
*black, slate gray, cream-colored, white on breast and paws
acceptable* **Life Expectancy:** *12 to 15 years and longer*

Japan Chin

Also: *Chin*

History: The Chin was to Japan as the Pekingese was to China. It surely was related to the short-nosed breeds from China. A small, rotund dog with silky fur, which had its place in the sleeves of noble ladies' kimonos. A pair of Chin dogs first went to Germany in 1880 as a gift from the Japanese Empress to Empress Augusta.

Character: A lively, receptive indoor dog that is gentle with its humans and forms a close bond with them. It gets along very well with other dogs. Easy to train and tractable, very watchful without being aggressive.

Living Conditions: These dogs get along fine indoors. Even several Chins get along fine together. They like to play and take varied walks.

Health: Hydrocephalus (water on the brain), dry eyes (inadequate supply of tears), epilepsy, hypothyroidism.

Appropriate for: Beginners

Training: 🐾
City: 🐾
Family: 🐾 🐾
Care: 🐾 🐾 🐾 🐾 🐾
Activity Level: 🐾 🐾 🐾

QUICK INFO FIC Group 9 / No. 206: *Companion and Toy Dogs* **Country of Origin:** *Japan* **Size:** *approximately 11 inches (28 cm)* **Weight:** *approximately 6.6 pounds (3 kg)* **Fur:** *thick, long, silky* **Color:** *white with red or black markings, symmetrical facial markings* **Life Expectancy:** *up to 15 years*

Japan Spitz

Also: *Nihon Supittsu*

History: Still a very rare dog, which evidently is descended from the Nordic Spitz. However, opinion is divided on that. One thing for sure is that this is a relatively new breed that existed around 1900 in Japan. The similarity in physique and disposition to the German Spitz is unmistakable, so it may also be an offshoot of that dog.

Character: A friendly dog that likes children; it is watchful, but doesn't bark, as the German Spitz does. It is quick to learn and easy to train. The most important thing is its lack of hunting instinct.

Living Conditions: A good choice even for small homes. It has no great need to run, but likes regular walks and longer hikes.

Health: Displaced patella, others unknown.

Appropriate for: Beginners

Training:	🐾
City:	🐾
Family:	🐾
Care:	🐾🐾🐾🐾🐾
Activity Level:	🐾🐾🐾

QUICK INFO **FIC Group 5/No. 262:** *Spitz and Primitive Types* **Country of Origin:** *Japan* **Size:** *12–15 inches (30–38 cm)* **Weight:** *approximately 11 pounds (5 kg)* **Fur:** *long, straight, erect, soft, thick undercoat* **Color:** *white* **Life Expectancy:** *10 to 12 years*

135

Kangal

History: In Turkey the only dogs that can be called Kangals are purebreds from Kangal itself or around the city of Sivas, and recorded in the registry for Kangal dogs. The former noble Kangal family from Sivas played an important role in the breeding of Kangals in Turkey for hundreds of years. The Kangal is distinguished from the Karabash by its pure breeding. It alone is considered a purebred in Turkey.

Training: 🐾 🐾 🐾 🐾
City: no
Family: 🐾 🐾 🐾 🐾 🐾
Care: 🐾
Activity Level: 🐾 🐾 🐾

Character: It is mistrustful of strangers, very watchful with a pronounced protective instinct. Not submissive, it takes the defense of its territory very seriously.

Living Conditions: Its protective instinct makes this dog reserved and distrustful with strangers, and it is highly stressed by the confusion of city living. Its personality and character make it a questionable candidate for pet status.

Health: HD.

Appropriate for: Specialists

QUICK INFO **FIC Group:** *Not recognized* **Country of Origin:** *Turkey* **Size:** *males 29–33.5 inches (74–85 cm), females 28–31 inches (71–79 cm)* **Weight:** *Males 110–150 pounds (50–68 kg), females 88–121 pounds (40–55 kg)* **Fur:** *short, thick* **Color:** *beige or brown with dark mask* **Life Expectancy:** *up to 15 years*

Karabash

History: Karabash means "black head"; in Turkey it is also called *Comar* or *Samson*. In contrast to the Kangal, which was bred by the upper classes from the Karabash and by and large was better nourished, the Karabash is the all-purpose dog of the Turkish farmers and shepherds.

Training: 🐾 🐾 🐾 🐾
City: no
Family: 🐾 🐾 🐾 🐾
Care: 🐾
Activity Level: 🐾 🐾 🐾

Character: The same as the Kangal. It is an unadulterated herding dog.

Living Conditions: Herding dogs sometimes don't make the best family companion dogs. They prefer country living to apartments in the city and their defensive instincts are deeply ingrained. For their happiness and peace of mind these dogs belong in a farm or ranch environment.

Health: HD.

Appropriate for: Specialists

QUICK INFO FIC Group: *Not recognized* **Country of Origin:** *Turkey* **Size:** *males 29–33.5 inches (74–85 cm), females 28–31 inches (71–79 cm)* **Weight:** *males 110–150 pounds (50–68 kg), females 88–121 pounds (40–55 kg)* **Fur:** *short and thick* **Color:** *beige or gray with dark mask or dark head* **Life Expectancy:** *12 to 15 years*

Karelian Bear Dog

Also: *Karjalankarhukoira*

History: You would not think from its size that this dog would dare to confront a bear on a hunt. Its task is not to kill the bear, elk, deer, wolf, lynx, or wild boar; rather it searches out and pursues the animal on its own, but silently. Only when it has the animal at bay does it bark.

Character: It is friendly with its family, but reserved with strangers. Aggressive with other dogs.

Living Conditions: This is a difficult dog to keep, even with continual training. The Karelian Bear Dog always tries to break free and hunt on its own. It is very difficult to introduce to dog sports.

Health: Very robust and healthy.

Appropriate for: Specialists

Training: 🐾🐾🐾🐾🐾
City: no
Family: 🐾🐾🐾🐾🐾
Care: 🐾🐾
Activity Level: 🐾🐾🐾🐾🐾

QUICK INFO **FIC Group 5/No. 48:** *Spitzes and Primitive Dogs* **Country of Origin:** *Finland* **Size:** *20–22.5 inches (52–57 cm)* **Weight:** *48–60 pounds (22–27 kg)* **Fur:** *thick, double, standing straight out with thick undercoat* **Color:** *black, preferably with light brown luster, with pure white markings* **Life Expectancy:** *12 to 15 years*

Kerry Blue Terrier

History: From county Kerry, a hardy breed that is capable of doing many things. The dogs are watchdogs, ratters and mousers, livestock drivers, hunters for badgers, rabbits, and birds, and outstanding retrievers.

Training: 🐾 🐾
City: 🐾 🐾 🐾 🐾 🐾
Family: 🐾 🐾 🐾
Care: 🐾 🐾 🐾 🐾 🐾
Activity Level: 🐾 🐾 🐾 🐾 🐾

Character: Intelligent and quick to learn. A good watchdog, but it rarely barks. It is apprehensive around strangers. It can be balky and moody. A beginner often doesn't know how to deal with its strong personality. An owner who trains with consistency will best appreciate this dog. It romps enthusiastically with other dogs.

Living Conditions: Although the British have clipped this dog for shows, it doesn't belong on the couch; instead, it needs lots of exercise in accord with its talents. If all of that is in place, it is a very interesting family dog.

Health: HD, entropion, tendency toward tumors.

Appropriate for: Experienced owners

QUICK INFO FIC Group 3/No. 3: *Terriers* **Country of Origin:** *Ireland* **Size:** *18.5 inches (47 cm)* **Weight:** *33–40 pounds (15–18 kg)* **Fur:** *silky, soft, thick, curly* **Color:** *blue, with or without black mask* **Life Expectancy:** *10 to 13 years*

King Charles Spaniel

Also: *Toy Spaniel*

History: One of Henry the Eighth's many wives brought the King Charles Spaniel with her in the thirteenth century. In contrast to the Cavalier King Charles (see page 76), this dog is smaller and has a shorter snout. The English kings Charles the First and Charles the Second are said to have paid more attention to their dogs than to the duties of their reign.

Character: This dog is strongly programmed to its humans. It is devoted and placid, and it rarely barks. Small, excitable children are not its preferred partners.

Living Conditions: Consistent training is essential. It shows its liveliness outdoors and likes to take long walks.

Health: Kneecap dislocation, eye and breathing problems, openings in the skull bones (fontanelles), hereditary heart problems.

Appropriate for: Beginners

Training: 🐾 🐾
City: 🐾
Family: 🐾 🐾
Care: 🐾 🐾 🐾 🐾 🐾
Activity Level: 🐾 🐾 🐾

QUICK INFO **FIC Group 9/No. 128:** *Companion and Toy Dogs* **Country of Origin:** *Great Britain* **Size:** *9–12 inches (22–30 cm)* **Weight:** *7.7–14.3 pounds (3.5–6.5 kg)* **Fur:** *rich, silky, long, straight with richly feathered legs* **Color:** *tricolor (formerly "Prince Charles"), white with red blotches, ruby (chestnut)* **Life Expectancy:** *9 to 15 years*

Komondor

History: This dog has been known since the sixteenth century as the Hungarian Shepherd; its job was to ensure the safety of the livestock. Its coat is made up of curtain-like, pendant, matted strings, which protected

Training: 🐾 🐾 🐾 🐾
City: no
Family: 🐾 🐾 🐾 🐾 🐾
Care: 🐾 🐾 🐾 🐾 🐾
Activity Level: 🐾 🐾 🐾 🐾 🐾

it from wolf bites and all kinds of weather. The only thing that saved this dog from extinction was the interest of dog breeders.

Character: This is a calm, serious, self-assured dog that acts independently and without orders. It is a stranger to blind obedience, and thus its trainability is suspect.

Living Conditions: This dog's peculiar coat, its independence, and rather large size make it a challenge for all but experienced dog owners.

Health: HD, skin irritations and infections, entropion.

Appropriate for: Advanced specialists

QUICK INFO FIC Group 1/No. 53: *Sheepdogs and Cattle-dogs* **Country of Origin:** *Hungary* **Size:** *25 inches (63 cm)* **Weight:** *95–99 pounds (43–45 kg)* **Fur:** *strong, waterproof, double, consisting of long strings matted together* **Color:** *white* **Life Expectancy:** *approximately 10 years or more*

Kooikerhondje

History: The catching of wild ducks in Kojen with the help of a "Kojenjound" is a very long tradition in Holland: part of an open canal was covered over with wire mesh, and in an open canal with no covering tame ducks were raised and fed in association with the dog. When wild ducks rested during their migration, the dog ran along the bank, and the tame ducks in the covered section swam, for they usually were fed when the dog appeared. The wild ducks swam along into the trap and couldn't take off because of the wire covering.

Character: Nowadays the Kooikerhondje is a beloved companion dog, for it is intelligent, quick to learn, and easy to train.

Living Conditions: This dog is happy, lively, and alert. It doesn't like unruly children.

Health: No particular known diseases.

Appropriate for: Beginners

Training: 🐾
City: 🐾🐾
Family: 🐾🐾 🐾
Care: 🐾
Activity Level: 🐾🐾 🐾🐾

QUICK INFO **FIC Group 8/No. 314:** *Retrievers, Flushing Dogs, and Water Dogs* **Country of Origin:** *Netherlands* **Size:** *14–16 inches (35–40 cm)* **Weight:** *approximately 22 pounds (10 kg)* **Fur:** *medium long, fine, feathered front legs, tail, and ears* **Color:** *white with orange-red splotches* **Life Expectancy:** *approximately 12 years and longer*

Kromfohrlander

History: In 1945 Ilse Schleifenbaum randomly crossed a wirehaired Fox Terrier female with a presumed Breton Griffon and got a homogeneous litter of white and brown dogs. She was fascinated by their appearance and character, so she kept breeding them; in 1955 the breed became recognized as the Kromfohrlander.

Training: 🐾
City: 🐾
Family: 🐾 🐾
Care: 🐾
Activity Level: 🐾 🐾 🐾

Character: "This dog is a mixture of happiness and thoughtfulness. The Kromfohrlander is devoted without being submissive, faithful and reliable, strong-willed, without any major inclination toward obstinacy." (Ilse Schleifenbaum)

Living Conditions: This is a good watchdog and likes to bark. It gets along fine with older children. It doesn't run off, and it's a good candidate for agility. It needs a strong bond with its family, and active people who like to make things happen.

Health: Knee problems.

Appropriate for: Beginners

QUICK INFO FIC Group 9/No. 192: *Companion and Toy Dogs* **Country of Origin:** *Germany* **Size:** *15–18 inches (38–46 cm)* **Weight:** *22–35 pounds (10–16 kg)* **Fur:** *smooth or wirehaired* **Color:** *white with brown spots* **Life Expectancy:** *15 to 17 years*

Kuvasz

History: The name *Kuvasz* is Turkish and means *protector*. And that's just what this dog has been doing ever since the breed came into what is now Hungary with immigrant shepherds. In the Second World War and in 1956 during the Hungarian uprising, the Kuvasz in Hungary nearly died out, and their continuation depended on breeding stock from other countries.

Training: 🐾 🐾 🐾
City: no
Family: 🐾 🐾 🐾
Care: 🐾 🐾 🐾
Activity Level: 🐾 🐾 🐾

Character: This dog has a strong personality. It finds its rank in its family only through regular training starting in puppyhood. It is a pleasant housemate and a reliable watchdog and defender.

Living Conditions: The Kuvasz needs plenty of room and regular exercise. It places high demands on its master's leadership qualities.

Health: HD, skin problems, deafness.

Appropriate for: Experienced owners

QUICK INFO FIC Group 1/No. 54: *Sheepdogs and Cattledogs* **Country of Origin:** *Hungary* **Size:** *27.5–30 inches (70–76 cm)* **Weight:** *approximately 115 pounds (52 kg)* **Fur:** *long, double, slightly wavy or lying flat against the body* **Color:** *white or ivory* **Life Expectancy:** *up to 10 years*

Labrador Retriever

History: The Labrador–whether in yellow, chocolate, or black–is one of the most versatile companion dogs currently in existence. It comes from the south of Newfoundland and is bred for work in the water. The

Training:	🐾
City:	🐾
Family:	🐾
Care:	🐾
Activity Level:	🐾 🐾 🐾

English refined the breed by crossing it with a pointer. This is a good hunting dog, and an outstanding drug sniffer, rescue dog, avalanche dog, and seeing-eye dog.

Character: An even-tempered dog with an outstanding nature. It is devoted, and doesn't run away or hunt on its own. It is patient and playful with children, and affectionate.

Living Conditions: In spite of all its good qualities, this dog needs consistent training. Its gluttony has to be kept under control; otherwise it becomes lazy and bored. A problem-free companion dog in public.

Health: HD, elbow dysplasia, PRA, epilepsy, glaucoma, cataracts, dwarfism entropion, hypothyroidism, diabetes, and others.

Appropriate for: Beginners

QUICK INFO **FIC Group 8/No. 122:** *Retrievers, Flushing Dogs, and Water Dogs* **Country of Origin:** *Great Britain* **Size:** *21–24 inches (54–62 cm)* **Weight:** *55–80 pounds (25–36 kg)* **Fur:** *hard, thick topcoat with waterproof undercoat* **Color:** *black, chocolate, yellow* **Life Expectancy:** *11 to 15 years*

Laekenois

History: This fourth Belgian shepherd breed was bred by a shepherd family in the park of Laeken Castle. The wiry-haired Laeken is often overlooked because of the popularity of other Belgian dogs (see pages 124,

Training: 🐾🐾
City: no
Family: 🐾🐾
Care: 🐾
Activity Level: 🐾🐾🐾🐾🐾

154, and 213) and is not encountered very frequently. Perhaps people are not impressed by its unkempt appearance.
Character: In addition to its fine herding abilities, it is an alert watchdog and a fearless defender. It is more consistent and calmer than some of its perpetually agile and somewhat nervous cousins.
Living Conditions: This robust herding dog much prefers to be outdoors, but it still enjoys a close bonding as a family member. It loves to run, so it has to be kept busy and individually given lots of exercise.
Health: Hip joint dysplasia (HD), epilepsy.
Appropriate for: Experienced owners

QUICK INFO **FIC Group 1/No. 15:** *Sheepdogs and Cattledogs* **Country of Origin:** *Belgium* **Size:** *23–24 inches (58–62 cm)* **Weight:** *62–70 pounds (28–32 kg)* **Fur:** *2.5 inches (6 cm) long, tough, rough, unkempt* **Color:** *reddish brown* **Life Expectancy:** *10 to 12 years*

Lakeland Terrier

History: This dog bears a close resemblance to the Welsh Terrier (see page 220), but is not related to it, but rather to the Border, Bedlington, and Dandie Dinmont Terriers. Its job was to hunt foxes and grapple with them bodily. Nowadays it is seldom used for hunting, and is kept mostly indoors, but it's still a Terrier.

Training: 🐾 🐾
City: 🐾
Family: 🐾
Care: 🐾 🐾 🐾 🐾
Activity Level: 🐾 🐾 🐾 🐾 🐾

Character: This dog is friendly and has a good disposition, and it gets along fine with children. It needs consistent training, since it can also be a little resolute. Overall it is calmer and more sensible than many other Terriers.

Living Conditions: It has a strong hunting instinct. Its high voice may sometimes irritate the neighbors. It needs regular trimming.

Health: Lens luxation, undershot jaw, cryptorchidism.

Appropriate for: Beginners

QUICK INFO FIC Group 3/No. 70: *Terriers* **Country of Origin:** *Great Britain* **Size:** *approximately 14 inches (36 cm)* **Weight:** *males 17 pounds (7.7 kg), females 15 pounds (6.8 kg)* **Fur:** *hard, thick, waterproof, with thick, soft undercoat* **Color:** *blue with tan, black and tan, red, wheat red, grizzled red, liver, blue and black* **Life Expectancy:** *often over 15 years*

Landseer

History: In the eighteenth century Landseers and Newfoundlands (see page 165) were still a single breed. When Sir Edwin Landseer created a black and white Newfoundland, it was named for him. When this breed ceased to exist, it was reconstituted from Newfoundlands with the help of Swiss breeders. In the United States it is a color variety of the Newfoundland.

Training:	🐾
City:	no
Family:	🐾
Care:	🐾 🐾 🐾
Activity Level:	🐾 🐾 🐾

Character: Regardless of what rival breeders think, the Landseer, like the Newfoundland, is a big bundle of charm, faithfulness, good disposition, and reliability. It has a great love for its human.

Living Conditions: This dog needs plenty of room in the house and yard. It likes comfortable, moderate walks. It enjoys swimming.

Health: HD, knee problems, heart disease, entropion, dewclaws (see page 19), bloat.

Appropriate for: Beginners

QUICK INFO FIC Group 2/No. 226: *Pinschers and Schnauzers, Molossians, and Swiss Mountain and Cattledogs* **Country of Origin:** *Germany and Switzerland* **Size:** *26–31.5 inches (67–80 cm)* **Weight:** *132–154 pounds (60–70 kg)* **Fur:** *long, heavy, thick* **Color:** *white with black blotches, head always black* **Life Expectancy:** *approximately 10 years*

Leonberger

History: This dog got its name from the city of Leonberg. Heinrich Essig, a city councilman from Leonberg, wanted to create a dog that looked like the lion in the Leonberg city coat of arms. We don't know for sure which breeds he crossed, but St. Bernard, Landseer, and Pyrenees Mountain Dog were part of the mix. Many people with name and status wanted to own this dog, including Otto von Bismarck, Empress Sissi, and Richard Wagner.

Training: 🐾🐾
City: no
Family: 🐾
Care: 🐾🐾🐾
Activity Level: 🐾🐾🐾

Character: Nowadays the Leonberger is a calm, composed dog that's a good watchdog, but which doesn't bark much. It is confident, but it also needs a lot of affection.

Living Conditions: This dog needs plenty of room and is not particularly fond of running, but likes to go for walks.

Health: HD, cartilage defects during growth, knee problems, dewclaws (see page 19), throat constriction.

Appropriate for: Beginners

QUICK INFO FIC Group 2/No. 145: *Pinschers and Schnauzers, Molossians, and Swiss Mountain and Cattledogs* **Country of Origin:** *Germany* **Size:** *30–31.5 inches (76–80 cm)* **Weight:** *over 88 pounds (40 kg)* **Fur:** *fairly long, thick, medium soft, waterproof* **Color:** *tawny, gold to reddish brown, sandy with black mask* **Life Expectancy:** *under 10 years*

Lhasa Apso

History: This very old breed was kept at Tibetan Temple sites as a watchdog. It is friendly but somewhat reserved with strangers.

Character: It doesn't want to be spoiled as a lap dog. It is proud and confident and wants to be taken seriously as a dog. It reacts to pampering with bad behavior. It is devoted and tender with its family, but isn't the best dog for boisterous little children. It always wants to know who the master of the house is; otherwise it will take over.

Training: 🐾 🐾
City: 🐾
Family: 🐾 🐾
Care: 🐾 🐾 🐾 🐾 🐾
Activity Level: 🐾 🐾 🐾

Living Conditions: A good indoor dog, but it also likes fairly long walks, and not just when it's sunny out. Coat care is very time consuming and essential; otherwise tangles will result.

Health: Eye and kidney problems, HD.

Appropriate for: Beginners

QUICK INFO FIC Group 9/No. 227: *Companion and Toy Dogs* **Country of Origin:** *Tibet (Great Britain)* **Size:** *approximately 10 inches (25 cm)* **Weight:** *approximately 13–22 pounds (6–10 kg)* **Fur:** *long, heavy, straight, and fairly stiff, with moderate undercoat* **Color:** *all colors including multicolored* **Life Expectancy:** *approximately 12 years and above*

Little Lion Dog

Also: *Lowchen, Petit chien lion*

History: For centuries this was the classic lapdog for noble ladies, and the dogs also lay around the feet of noblemen. The clipped hindquarters resembling a lion helped give this dog its name. The breed sank into oblivion—perhaps also because of this unique shearing—and had to be rebuilt from a very small gene pool.

Training: 🐾 🐾
City: 🐾
Family: 🐾
Care: 🐾 🐾 🐾
Activity Level: 🐾 🐾 🐾 🐾 🐾

Character: A lively, always pleasant, tractable dog that is good with children and has a pronounced taste for running and playing. In its family it is affectionate and cuddly, but it's somewhat reserved with strangers. It is alert, but it doesn't bark a lot.

Living Conditions: This dog will fit into the smallest city apartment as long as it can burn off calories on its beloved walks.

Health: Teeth problems, kneecap dislocation (rare).

Appropriate for: Beginners

QUICK INFO FIC Group 9/No. 223: *Companion and Toy Dogs* **Country of Origin:** *France* **Size:** *12.5 inches (32 cm)* **Weight:** *11 pounds (5 kg)* **Fur:** *long, wavy, silky soft but coarse* **Color:** *all colors except all brown, one color, and mottled* **Life Expectancy:** *over 12 years*

Lundehund

Also: *Norsk Lundehund, Norwegian Lundehund*

Training: 🐾 🐾
City: 🐾 🐾 🐾 🐾 🐾
Family: 🐾 🐾
Care: 🐾
Activity Level: 🐾 🐾 🐾 🐾 🐾

History: For centuries the Lundehund was trained to hunt Atlantic puffins, which they caught live in their holes in the cliffs by the sea. It thus developed special physical traits that no other dog has: it has five instead of four toes and two sturdy dewclaws for a secure hold in the cliffs. It can close up its ears to keep out mud, and its front legs join the body at a ninety-degree angle.

Character: Since there are not many of these dogs, we can only infer that it's probably not a good choice as a companion dog.

Living Conditions: Only real dog afficionados who can provide activity and living conditions appropriate to the breed should own such a special dog.

Health: Nothing is known about particular diseases.

Appropriate for: Specialized owners

QUICK INFO FIC Group 5/No. 265: *Spitzes and Primitive Dogs* **Country of Origin:** *Norway* **Size:** *12.5–15 inches (32–38 cm)* **Weight:** *13.2–17.6 pounds (6–8 kg)* **Fur:** *medium short, thick, waterproof* **Color:** *reddish brown with black hair tips, black or gray with white markings, white with dark markings* **Life Expectancy:** *over 10 years*

Magyar Vizsla

Also: *Hungarian Pointer*

History: A beautiful, versatile pointer that belongs to Hungary much as the Bernese Mountain Dog belongs to Switzerland. This breed was created as early as the eighteenth century by crossing Turkish hunting dogs with Pointers and German Shorthairs. The Magyar Vizsla is a versatile hunting dog for modern hunting.

Training: 🐾
City: 🐾🐾🐾🐾🐾
Family: 🐾
Care: 🐾
Activity Level: 🐾🐾🐾🐾🐾

Character: This dog is tractable and focused on its owner, devoted, and intelligent. It is very calm and obedient in the house and as a companion dog. It has plenty of tolerance for children.

Living Conditions: This very talented hunting dog is a good companion dog, but it really needs a good substitute for hunting; otherwise it may develop psychological problems. It can become intensively involved in dog sports, such as agility and other competitions, with no danger of overtaxing it.

Health: A healthy dog.

Appropriate for: Experienced owners

QUICK INFO **FIC Group 7/No. 57:** *Pointers* **Country of Origin:** *Hungary* **Size:** *22.5–25 inches (57–64 cm)* **Weight:** *48–66 pounds (22–30 kg)* **Fur:** *short, smooth, thick, close, shiny, with no undercoat* **Color:** *dark flaxen color* **Life Expectancy:** *14 to 15 years*

Malinois

Also: *Belgian Shepherd*

History: This is the shorthaired Belgian shepherd dog, and it comes from the region around Malines. In recent years dog sport enthusiasts and the police have discovered its usefulness for special tasks. In police work there is no quicker dog than the Malinois in defending against attack or in grabbing suspects.

Training: 🐾
City: 🐾 🐾 🐾 🐾
Family: 🐾
Care: 🐾
Activity Level: 🐾 🐾 🐾 🐾 🐾

Character: In the hands of an experienced dog sports person, this dog is also well suited as a house and family dog. Obedient and robust, it can often be quite sensitive despite its outstanding protective abilities.

Living Conditions: This dog needs lots of activity that also develops its intelligence. It finds exercise merely for the sake of defeating boredom. Following scents, obedience, nimbleness exercises, and agility every other day is much more to its liking.

Health: HD and (rarely) epilepsy.

Appropriate for: Experienced owners

QUICK INFO **FIC Group 1/No. 15:** *Sheepdogs and Cattledogs* **Country of Origin:** *Belgium* **Size:** *23–24 inches (58–62 cm)* **Weight:** *50–70 pounds (22.5–32 kg)* **Fur:** *short, thick, double* **Color:** *red to fawn with black mask* **Life Expectancy:** *10 to 14 years*

Maltese

History: This breed existed as early as ancient Rome and Greece, and it is among the very oldest of dog breeds. Later on in the French royal court these dogs delighted noble ladies and gentlemen as lap- and bed dogs. The

Training: 🐾 🐾
City: 🐾
Family: 🐾
Care: 🐾 🐾 🐾 🐾 🐾
Activity Level: 🐾 🐾 🐾

Maltese is the best known and the most beloved of the Bichons.

Character: Malteses are intelligent, lively, and quick to learn, and they follow their owner like a shadow. They are alert, but they don't bark endlessly.

Living Conditions: The Maltese likes to go for walks, and generally is no problem in public. Its beautiful, very long, and very heavy coat requires extremely time-consuming care.

Health: Teeth problems, kneecap dislocation, deafness, blindness, monorchism (only one testicle).

Appropriate for: Beginners

QUICK INFO **FIC Group 9/No. 65:** *Companion and Toy Dogs* **Country of Origin:** *Italy* **Size:** *8–10 inches (20–25 cm)* **Weight:** *4–6.6 pounds (1.8–3 kg)* **Fur:** *long, silky, abundant* **Color:** *pure white, pale ivory permissible* **Life Expectancy:** *approximately 13 years*

Manchester Terrier

History: This dog originated in the port sections of Liverpool and Manchester in England, where the Black and Tan Terrier, as it was then known, proved its worth by eliminating rats. By crossing with a whippet, it acquired an elegant appearance and became a favorite show dog.

Training: 🐾🐾
City: 🐾
Family: 🐾
Care: 🐾
Activity Level: 🐾🐾🐾

Character: This is a lively and active dog. Indoors it is clean and friendly and gets along well with well-mannered children. It is quick to learn and easy to train.

Living Conditions: Even though this dog likes exercise, it doesn't need to be kept busy all the time. It's a problem-free companion on walks. Because of its pleasant and undemanding nature, this healthy and steadfast Terrier will find more friends in the future.

Health: Entropion, glaucoma, epilepsy.

Appropriate for: Beginners

QUICK INFO FIC Group 3/No. 71: *Terriers* **Country of Origin:** *Great Britain* **Size:** *15–16 inches (38–41 cm)* **Weight:** *11–22 pounds (5–10 kg)* **Fur:** *short, thick, tight, shiny, doesn't feel soft* **Color:** *black and tan* **Life Expectancy:** *12 to 15 years*

Maremma Sheepdog

Also: *Maremma-Abruzzese Sheepdog, Cane da pastore Maremmano-Abruzzese*

Training:	🐾 🐾
City:	no
Family:	🐾 🐾
Care:	🐾 🐾 🐾
Activity Level:	🐾 🐾 🐾

History: In the middle of the thirteenth century, Mongols brought Asiatic mastiffs with them to Europe. In central Italy these powerful animals were crossed with dogs from the Abruzzi and Maremma regions. Ever since then, these white herding dogs have been protecting flocks from wolves.

Character: A confident, independent, decisive herd protector that is friendly and undemanding in the family. It is very quick to learn and intelligent. Its quickness to defend can sometimes cause problems.

Living Conditions: These dogs are very well suited to life outdoors. They are too big for indoors, although they enjoy bonding with the family. An apartment or a house with a small yard is not the best kind of arrangement.

Health: HD, possibly other skeletal problems.

Appropriate for: Experienced owners

QUICK INFO **FIC Group 1/No. 201:** *Sheepdogs and Cattledogs* **Country of Origin:** *Italy* **Size:** *males 25.5–28.75 inches (65–73 cm), females 24–26.75 inches (60–68 cm)* **Weight:** *approximately 114.5 pounds (52 kg)* **Fur:** *long, slightly wavy and rather hard with thick undercoat* **Color:** *white* **Life Expectancy:** *8 to 10 years*

Mastiff

History: The Celts and Normans brought their massive dogs with them to Britain; they are the originators of the mastiff. The goal was to produce larger hunting and guard dogs. The Mastiff was in turn the

Training: 🐾🐾
City: no
Family: 🐾🐾🐾
Care: 🐾🐾
Activity Level: 🐾🐾🐾

point of departure for many large breeds, such as the German Mastiff, the Bull Mastiff, and the Newfoundland.

Character: Friendly, even tempered, and sincere. It has an inborn guard reflex, but is not unnecessarily aggressive. Even with regular and consistent training, it is not always obedient. It is loving and well balanced.

Living Conditions: This dog needs adequate room in the house; even the yard should be big enough for it to pull its patrol duties conscientiously.

Health: HD, joint problems, ectropion, dewclaws (see page 19), infections in skin folds, bloat, elbow dysplasia.

Appropriate for: Experienced owners

QUICK INFO FIC Group 2/No. 264: *Pinscher and Schnauzers, Molossians, and Swiss Mountain and Cattledogs* **Country of Origin:** *Great Britain* **Size:** *up to 31.5 inches (80 cm) and unfortunately even larger* **Weight:** *often up to 198 pounds (90 kg)* **Fur:** *short and close* **Color:** *apricot, silver, dun, dark striped, black mask* **Life Expectancy:** *7 to 10 years*

Medium-sized Poodle

History: The poodle is among the oldest dog breeds and is descended from the old water dogs. Poodles are found in portraits dating from the Baroque and Rococo eras as companions for noble ladies. For a long time this dog had to be clipped according to French standards (the Lion cut). Around 1950, when the new cut prevailed after long resistance, the miniature poodle began its victory run as the most popular dog.

Training: 🐾
City: 🐾
Family: 🐾
Care: 🐾 🐾 🐾 🐾 🐾
Activity Level: 🐾 🐾 🐾

Character: Intelligent, happy, affectionate, adaptable, and easy to train. It likes well-behaved and well-mannered children.

Living Conditions: The Miniature Poodle is easily trained with love and consistency. If a heavy hand is used, it may respond with stubbornness and moodiness that will lead to an irritable and unhappy pet.

Health: HD, epilepsy, skin problems, susceptibility to cataracts, PRA.

Appropriate for: Beginners

QUICK INFO FIC Group 9/No. 172: *Companion and Toy Dogs* **Country of Origin:** *France* **Size:** *14–18 inches (35–45 cm)* **Weight:** *26 pounds (12 kg)* **Fur:** *double, thick, woolly, very curly* **Color:** *black, white, brown, silver, and apricot* **Life Expectancy:** *up to 15 years or more*

Miniature Pinscher

History: Originally, the Miniature Pinscher, which was bred from the German Pinscher, was an enterprising ratter. Today it is purely a companion dog, and it has its own circle of fans.

Training: 🐾🐾
City: 🐾
Family: 🐾
Care: 🐾
Activity Level: 🐾🐾🐾

Character: This dog is more robust than it appears to be. It is a lively, intelligent, and devoted companion for adults and adolescents, a strong, energetic, and active terrier that likes to be heard.

Living Conditions: This dog's greatest danger is from small children who should be taught never to pick up or carry this little dog because its bones are fragile. It should receive plenty of kind, consistent training and warm housing, but it likes walks and only needs a sweater in especially inclement weather.

Health: Heart and blood vessel abnormalities, kidney stones, displaced patella, PRA, Legg-Perthes' disease.

Appropriate for: Beginners

QUICK INFO FIC Group 2/No. 185: *Pinschers, Schnauzers, Molossians, and Swiss Mountain and Cattledogs* **Country of Origin:** *Germany* **Size:** *10–12 inches (25–30 cm)* **Weight:** *8.8 pounds (4 kg)* **Fur:** *short, thick, shiny* **Color:** *black and liver, shiny red, chocolate and rust colors* **Life Expectancy:** *13 to 14 years*

Miniature Poodle

History: With Poodles there is a choice of four sizes (see pages 159, 211, and 217). In the 1950s to the 1970s, when hysterical mass breeding began, the Miniature Poodle was bred with psychological defects, much to its detriment. Nowadays, since it is no longer so new to the scene, it is recovering in the hands of responsible breeders.

Training: 🐾
City: 🐾
Family: 🐾
Care: 🐾 🐾 🐾 🐾 🐾
Activity Level: 🐾 🐾 🐾

Character: These dogs are cheerful, playful, and exceptionally intelligent. They like it when someone teaches them something, and they like human company.

Living Conditions: Because of their manageable size, Miniature Poodles are the ideal indoor dog; they don't shed as long as they are trimmed regularly. They are clean and friendly when they are socialized properly.

Health: Epilepsy, skin problems, susceptibility to glaucoma, PRA.

Appropriate for: Beginners

QUICK INFO FIC Group 9/No. 172: *Companion and Toy Dogs* **Country of Origin:** *France* **Size:** *11–14 inches (28–35 cm)* **Weight:** *15.5 pounds (7 kg)* **Fur:** *double, abundant, woolly, very curly* **Color:** *black, white, brown, silver, and apricot* **Life Expectancy:** *14 to 17 years*

Miniature Schnauzer

History: The Miniature Schnauzer was first shown as a separate breed in 1899. Previously it was barely distinguishable from the Affenpinscher (see page 28). But people wanted an exact, miniature replica of the

Training:	🐾 🐾
City:	🐾
Family:	🐾 🐾
Care:	🐾 🐾 🐾 🐾
Activity Level:	🐾 🐾 🐾

Schnauzer. That has turned out well to this day. Mass breeding has contributed some character defects and hereditary diseases.

Character: This is a confident companion dog. As a fearless go-getter, it is also a good watchdog, and a very loud one. It is a happy companion on hikes.

Living Conditions: Its fur should be trimmed regularly. Its training must begin early and be carried out consistently. This is also an ideal dog for older people.

Health: PRA and other eye problems, bladder stones, dry eye (inadequate tear flow), epilepsy.

Appropriate for: Beginners

QUICK INFO **FIC Group 2/No. 183:** *Pinschers and Schnauzers, Molossians, and Swiss Mountain and Cattledogs* **Country of Origin:** *Germany* **Size:** *12–14 inches (30–36 cm)* **Weight:** *13–14.5 pounds (6–7 kg)* **Fur:** *rough, wiry, hard, thick undercoat* **Color:** *black, white, salt and pepper, black and silver* **Life Expectancy:** *approximately 14 years*

Mudi

Also: *Hungarian Mudi*

History: Even in Hungary the Mudi is a rare breed. In other places it is practically unknown. Because of work, it never managed to make it as a show dog. It herds cattle, horses, and sheep, and in its free time it also keeps the barnyard free of rats and mice. There are many variations in appearance, for it is continually crossed with working dogs that have no pedigree.

Character: The Mudi is intelligent, quick to learn, and watchful, but it's not as noisy as the Puli or the Pumi (see pages 185 and 186).

Living Conditions: Even though this dog has to get plenty of activity to satisfy its need for exercise and its intelligence, it also enjoys a life of luxury in the city.

Health: Overall these dogs are bred to be healthy.

Appropriate for: Beginners

Training: 🐾
City: 🐾 🐾 🐾 🐾
Family: 🐾
Care: 🐾
Activity Level: 🐾 🐾 🐾 🐾

QUICK INFO FIC Group 1/No. 238: *Sheepdogs and Cattle-dogs* **Country of Origin:** *Hungary* **Size:** *13–18.5 inches (34–47 cm)* **Weight:** *17.5–29 pounds (8–13 kg)* **Fur:** *abundant, thick, waterproof, with undercoat* **Color:** *black, rarely white, brown, ash, blue merle* **Life Expectancy:** *over 12 years*

Neapolitan Mastiff

Also: *Mastino Napoletano*

History: This breed is descended from the Molossians. In the 1940s, the modern Neapolitan Mastiff was nearly ruined by inappropriate breeding that produced an overly aggressive, dangerous breed.

Training:	🐾🐾🐾
City:	no
Family:	🐾🐾🐾
Care:	🐾🐾
Activity Level:	🐾🐾🐾

Character: Today, conscientious breeders are bringing out the more tractable and trainable characteristics and emphasizing the breed's positive points. The dog is quite loyal and loving to its owners. It responds well to early and continued leadership training and socialization.

Living Conditions: This dog should be kept only by people who are very skilled at handling dogs, and who will deal with the dog responsibly.

Health: HD, ectropion, cartilage problems during growth, misaligned bones, elbow dysplasia, osteochondrosis (bone deterioration), and arthritis. This dog salivates a lot.

Appropriate for: Specialists

QUICK INFO FIC Group 2/No.197: *Pinschers and Schnauzers, Molossians, and Swiss Mountain and Cattledogs* **Country of Origin:** *Italy* **Size:** *25.5–30 inches (65–75 cm)* **Weight:** *up to 154 pounds (70 kg)* **Fur:** *short and thick, hard* **Color:** *blue-gray, black, brown, reddish yellow, stag red, striped* **Life Expectancy:** *under 10 years*

Newfoundland

History: English fishermen brought
this dog from Newfoundland and
turned it into a helper. These dogs
are so adapted to aquatic life that
they even have webbed feet. They
have made a name for themselves as
water rescue dogs. When they are young they are amusing
because of their bear-like clumsiness.

Training: 🐾 🐾
City: no
Family: 🐾
Care: 🐾 🐾 🐾
Activity Level: 🐾 🐾 🐾

Character: This is a very lovable, calm, and adaptable dog. It
is neither ferocious nor nippy.

Living Conditions: This dog likes a large yard or a courtyard
so it can wander about, for it prefers to be outdoors. Since it
adores swimming, it absolutely needs opportunities to get
into the water. Unfortunately it salivates quite a bit.

Health: HD, ectropion, entropion, heart diseases, knee problems, dewclaws (see page 19), bloat.

Appropriate for: Beginners

QUICK INFO FIC Group 2/No. 50: *Pinschers and Schnauzers, Molossians, and Swiss Mountain and Cattledogs*
Country of Origin: *Canada* **Size:** *25.5–27.5 inches (65–70 cm)*
Weight: *99–150 pounds (45–68 kg)* **Fur:** *long, heavy, flat,
slightly wavy, thick, greasy undercoat* **Color:** *black, brown,
black and white* **Life Expectancy:** *approximately 10 years*

Norfolk Terrier

History: The Norfolk Terrier and Norwich Terrier breeds (see page 168) come from the same roots. Whereas the Norfolk's ears hang down, the Norwich's are erect. Neither the tail nor the ears of the Norwich are docked. Both breeds were tough, intense rat catchers. The two breeds have been recognized separately since 1964.

Character: The Norfolk is adaptable, active, and very curious. In contrast to other Terriers, it is easy to train. It is lively and robust, but also gentle and lovable, and patient with children.

Living Conditions: This dog always wants to be in the middle of things; that's no problem, for it is very confident, but not rowdy. The coarse hair needs trimming twice a year. It needs active owners with a good sense of humor.

Health: Eczema, dystocia.

Appropriate for: Beginners

Training: 🐾🐾
City: 🐾
Family: 🐾
Care: 🐾🐾🐾
Activity Level: 🐾🐾🐾🐾

QUICK INFO FIC Group 3/No. 72: *Terriers* **Country of Origin:** *Great Britain* **Size:** *10 inches (25 cm)* **Weight:** *11 pounds (5 kg)* **Fur:** *hard, wiry, straight, close, with thick undercoat* **Color:** *red, wheat, black and tan, grizzled* **Life Expectancy:** *over 10 years*

Norwegian Elkhound

Also: *Norsk Elghund gra*

History: The gray Norwegian Elkhound, which also exists as a separate breed in black, hunts elk silently and independently, and barks only when it corners the quarry. The gray Elkhound is Norway's national dog and is a common family dog. Today's standard has been recognized since the end of the nineteenth century.

Character: The Elkhound is friendly toward people and courageous. It has a loud voice, which it likes to use. This dog is good with children. It is watchful, but not prone to bite. It is easy to train, but because of its self-confidence it is not always totally obedient.

Living Conditions: This is no dog for small living conditions. It needs lots of exercise, and still its hunting instinct can lead to problems if ample exercise isn't provided.

Health: Cataracts, PRA, glaucoma.

Appropriate for: Experienced owners

Training:	🐾🐾
City:	no
Family:	🐾🐾🐾🐾
Care:	🐾🐾🐾
Activity Level:	🐾🐾🐾🐾🐾

QUICK INFO **FIC Group 5/No. 242:** *Spitz and Primitive Types* **Country of Origin:** *Norway* **Size:** *males 20 inches (52 cm), females 16 inches (40 cm)* **Weight:** *up to about 33 pounds (15 kg)* **Fur:** *thick, waterproof, woolly* **Color:** *various shades of gray* **Life Expectancy:** *10 to 12 years*

Norwich Terrier

History: Like its Norfolk Terrier cousin (see page 166), the Norwich Terrier was also used for hunting foxes and badgers. Students at Cambridge University used this dog as their mascot. In contrast to the Norfolk, it has small, erect ears. The Norwich is one of the smallest Terriers.

Training: 🐾 🐾
City: 🐾
Family: 🐾
Care: 🐾 🐾 🐾
Activity Level: 🐾 🐾 🐾 🐾 🐾

Character: This dog is small in stature, but in character it is tough, animated, confident, and sociable. It needs close bonding with people, is easy to train, and is free of aggression.

Living Conditions: This dog needs lots of activity; ideally it will learn a new trick every day. It poses no problems with other dogs on long walks, which it often withstands better than its handler. The Norwich Terrier needs light trimming twice a year.

Health: Overall, a healthy breed, except for difficulties at birth.

Appropriate for: Beginners

QUICK INFO FIC Group 3/No. 72: *Terriers* **Country of Origin:** *Great Britain* **Size:** *10–12 inches (25–30 cm)* **Weight:** *11 pounds (5 kg)* **Fur:** *hard, wiry, straight, tight, with thick undercoat* **Color:** *red, white, black and tan, grizzled* **Life Expectancy:** *over 10 years*

Nova Scotia Duck Tolling Retriever

History: This dog's origins and method of hunting are revealed in its name. The hunter lets a dog out of the blind to run back and forth on the shore until the curious ducks come close to the shore. Then he calls the dog to him, reveals himself to the ducks, which take to the air; the hunter shoots them, and the dog retrieves them. The Indians had used this rare hunting method against foxes even before the arrival of the settlers.

Training: 🐾
City: 🐾 🐾 🐾 🐾
Family: 🐾 🐾
Care: 🐾
Activity Level: 🐾 🐾 🐾

Character: The Toller is the smallest retriever. This very uncomplicated breed is lively, playful, easy to train, and obedient.

Living Conditions: A tractable Retriever that is also a good choice for competitive dog sports and agility

Health: HD, elbow dysplasia.

Appropriate for: Beginners

QUICK INFO **FIC Group 8/No. 312:** *Retrievers, Flushing Dogs, and Water Dogs* **Country of Origin:** *Canada* **Size:** *males 19–20 inches (48–51 cm), females 18–19 inches (45–48 cm)* **Weight:** *males 44–51 pounds (20–23 kg), females 37–44 pounds (17–20 kg)* **Fur:** *plain, fairly long* **Color:** *various shades of red or orange with white markings on head, breast, paws, and tail* **Life Expectancy:** *10 to 12 years*

Old English Sheepdog

Also: _Bobtail_

History: Originally a shaggy, robust, confident shepherd dog used for defending the herd. Nowadays it is a highly styled and pampered show dog.

Training: 🐾 🐾
City: 🐾 🐾 🐾 🐾
Family: 🐾 🐾
Care: 🐾 🐾 🐾 🐾 🐾
Activity Level: 🐾 🐾 🐾 🐾

Character: A lively, intelligent, and happy dog with a great, even disposition. It can also be resolute, so it needs early and continued but loving and patient training.

Living Conditions: Even if you are a fanatic about caring for your dog and have nothing else to do with your time, you won't be able to keep this dog's coat from becoming matted. Many Bobtail owners regularly shear their dogs, which makes a tremendous difference to this happy dog's quality of life.

Health: HD, entropion, umbilical hernia, deafness, leg problems, blood disease, cataracts, bloat.

Appropriate for: Experienced owners

QUICK INFO **FIC Group 1/No. 16:** _Sheepdogs and Cattledogs_ **Country of Origin:** _Great Britain_ **Size:** _22–23 inches (56–58 cm)_ **Weight:** _66 pounds (30 kg)_ **Fur:** _thick, soft, long_ **Color:** _all shades of gray, blue, and blue-merle with or without white markings_ **Life Expectancy:** _10 to 15 years_

Otterhound

History: Among hunting dogs, the Otterhound is a pure specialist. During the Middle Ages it was used in packs to hunt feisty otters, which it followed to their den by swimming. It thus had to become an outstanding swimmer, and it still is. Mud bothers it even less than water. Since otters are no longer hunted, the Otterhound is out of work.

Training: 🐾
City: no
Family: 🐾 🐾 🐾 🐾
Care: 🐾 🐾
Activity Level: 🐾 🐾 🐾 🐾 🐾

Character: For a true hunting dog, it is sociable, friendly, and submissive. Once it sniffs water, though, it can become exceptionally independent. It is not deterred even by ice-cold water in the winter.

Living Conditions: In the house it is calm, and even though it is watchful, it is not vicious. Because of its passion for hunting, it's less comfortable as a companion dog.

Health: HD, skin problems, elbow dysplasia.

Appropriate for: Experienced owners

QUICK INFO FIC Group 6/No. 294: *Scent Hounds and Related Breeds* **Country of Origin:** *Great Britain* **Size:** *24–26 inches (60–67 cm)* **Weight:** *88–106 pounds (40–48 kg)* **Fur:** *greasy, rough, shaggy, thick undercoat* **Color:** *all colors for running dogs* **Life Expectancy:** *10 years or more*

Papillon

Also: *Butterfly Dog*

History: From the twelfth to the fourteenth centuries the upper crust of society could hardly imagine life without this dog. At that time they were dealing with the Phalene variety, which has drop ears (see page 176). Today's Papillon with erect ears arose only in the nineteenth century as the result of crossing with Chihuahuas and Spitzes.

Character: Intelligent, confident, affectionate, and lively little dogs. They mustn't be pampered.

Living Conditions: These dogs are fine when kept indoors, but they also like to go on walks. If they are not trained properly and consistently, they can turn into barking nuisances.

Health: Kneecap dislocation and epilepsy in the bloodline, deafness, entropion.

Appropriate for: Experienced owners

Training: 🐾 🐾
City: 🐾
Family: 🐾 🐾
Care: 🐾 🐾 🐾 🐾
Activity Level: 🐾 🐾 🐾

QUICK INFO FIC Group 9/No. 77: *Companion and Toy Dogs* **Country of Origin:** *France/Belgium* **Size:** *8–11.5 inches (20–29 cm)* **Weight:** *8.8–10 pounds (4–4.5 kg)* **Fur:** *abundant, fine, silky; ears and hind legs well feathered, thick ruff* **Color:** *all colors permissible on a white background; predominantly white on body, colored head with blaze* **Life Expectancy:** *12 to 15 years*

Parson Jack Russell Terrier

History: In the mid-1800s an English hunter and minister named Russell bred multicolored white dogs only for performance, and without papers. Things continued that way until 1980 when the breeders got into the picture. In the meantime, this dog is recognized in two sizes.

Training: 🐾 🐾 🐾
City: 🐾 🐾 🐾
Family: 🐾 🐾
Care: 🐾 🐾
Activity Level: 🐾 🐾 🐾 🐾 🐾

Character: This terrier is a lively, energetic, and enterprising little dog. Like most terriers it has a mind of its own, which sometimes interferes with normal training. Its independence and drive is part of its personality.

Living Conditions: It's satisfied when it can follow its immediate interests freely but is hardly the companion for someone who wants a tractable and responsive pet.

Health: Lens dislocation and glaucoma may occur in wild strains.

Appropriate for: Knowledgeable owners

QUICK INFO FIC Group 3/No. 339: *Parson Russell Terrier (PR),* **No. 345:** *Jack Russell Terrier (JR)* **Country of Origin:** *Great Britain* **Size:** *PR: 13–14 inches (33–35 cm); JR: 10–12 inches (25–30 cm)* **Weight:** *PR: 8.8–17.6 pounds (4–8 kg); JR: 11–13.2 pounds (5–6 kg)* **Fur:** *both short, thick, smooth, shiny; also rough-haired, thick, hard, wiry* **Color:** *PR: white with brown and/or black markings on head and/or base of tail; JR: white with brown or black markings* **Life Expectancy:** *12 to 14 years*

Pekingese

Also: *Peking Palace Dog*

History: Supposedly these dogs accompanied Buddha and transformed themselves into lions in the face of danger. One thing for sure is that they were kept and bred only in the emperor's palace, and stealing one of these dogs resulted in a death sentence.

Training: 🐾 🐾 🐾 🐾
City: 🐾
Family: 🐾 🐾 🐾
Care: 🐾 🐾 🐾 🐾
Activity Level: 🐾 🐾 🐾

Character: This dog generously shares its friendliness. Its unpredictable nature can also lead to fits of anger, however. Veterinarians have tales to tell about its lightning-quick bite. This dog is self-assured and never subservient.

Living Conditions: You will get along with this dog as long as you acknowledge that it's a king and respect it. This dog is trained with difficulty. It has no great love of exercise, and it is happier as a one-person dog than as a family dog.

Health: Prolapsed eyeball, boils, hydrocephalus (water on the brain), dystocia, heart and blood vessel deformities, kidney stones, shortness of breath, cheilognathouranoschisis (cleft lip with cleft upper jaw and palate).

Appropriate for: Experienced owners

QUICK INFO FIC Group 9/ No. 207: *Companion and Toy Dogs* **Country of Origin:** *China* **Size:** *up to 10 inches (25 cm)* **Weight:** *10 to 13.2 pounds (4.5–6 kg)* **Fur:** *long, straight, abundant, pronounced mane around throat* **Color:** *all except albino and liver* **Life Expectancy:** *up to 14 years*

Petit Basset Griffon Vendéen

History: One of the four French short-legged dog breeds; these are not small dogs, but rather large dogs with short legs because of a hereditary shortening of the bones (chondrodystrophia fetalis). *Basset* comes from the French *bas*, meaning low or short.

Training: 🐾 🐾 🐾
City: 🐾 🐾 🐾 🐾
Family: 🐾
Care: 🐾 🐾
Activity Level: 🐾 🐾 🐾 🐾

Character: Gentle, always pleasant and uncomplicated. This dog is fairly easy to train, but not particularly obedient outdoors. Robust and sometimes as gruff as it appears.

Living Conditions: This dog requires supervision on walks, and sometimes restraint with a long leash, for it indulges passionately in hunting. Despite its small stature, it has a surprisingly loud voice.

Health: Largely free of inherited diseases.

Appropriate for: Experienced owners

QUICK INFO FIC Group 6/No. 67: *Scent Hounds and Related Breeds* **Country of Origin:** *France* **Size:** *13–15 inches (34–38 cm)* **Weight:** *33–44 pounds (15–20 kg)* **Fur:** *long, feels hard to the touch, thick undercoat* **Color:** *single color: rabbit or whitish gray; two-colored: white and orange, black and white, white and gray, white and tan; tricolor: white, black, and tan; white, rabbit, and tan; white, gray, and tan* **Life Expectancy:** *over 10 years*

Phalene

History: From the twelfth century up to the French Revolution, when it became nearly extinct, the Continental Dwarf Spaniel was the favorite lapdog. Only highly regarded people (such as Rubens) were eligible to own such dogs.

Training: 🐾🐾
City: 🐾
Family: 🐾🐾
Care: 🐾🐾🐾🐾
Activity Level: 🐾🐾🐾

Character: The Phalene is a serious, intelligent, confident tiny dog that is affectionate and loving. It's not a good choice for smaller children who are not well mannered.

Living Conditions: This dog doesn't need long walks, although it enjoys being outdoors. It needs plenty of consistent training; otherwise it turns into a prudish tyrant.

Health: Kneecap dislocation and epilepsy in the bloodline.

Appropriate for: Experienced owners

QUICK INFO FIC Group 9/No. 77: *Companion and Toy Dogs* **Country of Origin:** *France/Belgium* **Size:** *8–11.5 inches (20–29 cm)* **Weight:** *8.8–10 pounds (4–4.5 kg)* **Fur:** *abundant, silky fine; ears and hind legs well feathered, thick ruff on white background* **Color:** *all colors permissible; predominantly white on body, colored head with blaze* **Life Expectancy:** *12 to 15 years*

Pharaoh Hound

Also: *Kelb Tal Fenek*

History: In the Near East there were hunting dogs of the Pharaoh Hound type as early as five thousand years ago. At the time of Cleopatra, these dogs were distributed throughout the Mediterranean region by the Romans. This wonderful dog was rediscovered by breeders around 1960.

Training: 🐾🐾
City: 🐾🐾🐾🐾🐾
Family: 🐾🐾🐾
Care: 🐾
Activity Level: 🐾🐾🐾🐾🐾

Character: Friendly and loving; in contrast to other Sighthounds, it likes to be close to its human. This dog is easy to train, and always wants to be the center of attention.

Living Conditions: It doesn't hunt only with eyes and nose, but also with its sense of hearing. Thus, it needs to be kept under control outdoors. Any fence needs to take into account this dog's jumping ability. Indoors this dog is very clean and tidy.

Health: It is sensitive to many medications, insect bites, and drugs; gastrointestinal disorders.

Appropriate for: Experienced owners

QUICK INFO **FIC Group 5/No. 248:** *Spitz and Primitive Types* **Country of Origin:** *Malta (Great Britain)* **Size:** *21–25 inches (53–63 cm)* **Weight:** *44–55 pounds (20–25 kg)* **Fur:** *short, smooth, shiny* **Color:** *all colors from lustrous tan to chestnut with various white markings* **Life Expectancy:** *15 to 17 years*

177

Pinscher

Also: *German Pinscher*

History: Before the Schnauzer (see page 197) was "invented," there were only coarse- and smooth-haired Pinschers. If the Pinscher and Schnauzer Club had not been so involved with the Pinscher in 1956, it would have died out. It seems to be righting its course now, and its popularity is rising on the European continent.

Character: An attentive, robust, and trainable dog with a dashing temperament. It has a good disposition, is devoted, and likes to play. It is watchful, but is not a barker.

Living Conditions: This dog is very athletic, so it needs physical activity: dog competitions or agility.

Health: It has no serious health problems.

Appropriate for: Beginners

Training: 🐾
City: 🐾🐾
Family: 🐾🐾🐾
Care: 🐾
Activity Level: 🐾🐾🐾🐾

QUICK INFO FIC Group 2/No. 184: *Pinschers, Schnauzers, Molossians, and Swiss Mountain and Cattledogs* **Country of Origin:** *Germany* **Size:** *15.75–19 inches (40–48 cm)* **Weight:** *24–35 pounds (11–16 kg)* **Fur:** *short, hard, strong, shiny, close* **Color:** *all black, black with tan markings, russet to stag red, brown, chocolate, blue-gray with red or yellow markings, salt and pepper* **Life Expectancy:** *12 to 15 years*

Podenco Ibicenco

History: As a descendant of the ancient Pharaoh Hound (see page 177), the Podenco was kept on the Balearic Islands as a hunting dog mainly for rabbits. The Podenco hunts primarily with its eyes and nose, and it retrieves rabbits without damaging them.

Training:	🐾 🐾 🐾
City:	🐾 🐾 🐾 🐾 🐾
Family:	🐾 🐾
Care:	🐾
Activity Level:	🐾 🐾 🐾 🐾

Character: Indoors, the Podenco is especially clean and undemanding; however, it needs contact with people to keep from becoming withdrawn. At first this dog is reserved with strangers, and sometimes it even avoids them. It is very quick to learn.

Living Conditions: This dog is very quick outdoors, and its prey instinct requires careful oversight and appropriate measures. This dog is a tremendous jumper, even without a running start. Since the Podenco is a hunting dog, it needs lots of activity and exercise.

Health: Serious hereditary problems are very rare.

Appropriate for: Experienced owners

QUICK INFO FIC Group 5/No. 89: *Spitz and Primitive Types* **Country of Origin:** *Spain* **Size:** *22–26 inches (57–66 cm)* **Weight:** *42–50 pounds (19–22.5 kg)* **Fur:** *shorthair or rough hair, smooth, hard, thick, close* **Color:** *white and red, all white, or all red* **Life Expectancy:** *up to 13 years*

Pointer

Also: *English Pointer*
History: The specialized Pointer quickly beats the bushes mainly for game birds and is characterized by its typical pose. The configuration of today's pointer was established in the nineteenth century.

Training: 🐾
City: no
Family: 🐾 🐾
Care: 🐾
Activity Level: 🐾 🐾 🐾 🐾 🐾

Character: The Pointer is a passionate, spirited purebred hunting dog with lots of endurance and nerve. It is lovable and friendly.
Living Conditions: In spite of these positive character traits, it wants a hunting home if possible. Its need for work and exercise is so great that substitute activities often will not satisfy it.
Health: HD, skin problems, thyroid diseases, cataracts, PRA, entropion, deafness, epilepsy.
Appropriate for: Hunters and their families.

QUICK INFO FIC Group 7/No. 1: *Pointers* **Country of Origin:** *Great Britain* **Size:** *males 25–28 inches (63–71 cm), females 23–26 inches (58–66 cm)* **Weight:** *44–70.5 pounds (20–32 kg)* **Fur:** *fine, short, smooth and close, shiny* **Color:** *white with yellow, orange, liver, or black spots* **Life Expectancy:** *around 10 years*

Polski Owczarek Nizinny

Also: *Polish Lowland Sheepdog, PON*

History: After 1945 the PON was bred from Polish shepherd dogs used in the lowlands, and its name reflects that. The breed has been recognized since 1963, and it keeps winning over more and more fans. It has a very strong breed association, which so far has succeeded in keeping the PON from being commercialized.

Training: 🐾
City: 🐾 🐾 🐾
Family: 🐾 🐾
Care: 🐾 🐾 🐾 🐾 🐾
Activity Level: 🐾 🐾 🐾 🐾

Character: This is a reliable watchdog and guard dog, but it is not vicious. It is confident, and it participates enthusiastically in children's games. It demonstrates absolute loyalty and obedience with its recognized pack leader.

Living Conditions: As a former herding dog, the PON needs clear rules of conduct. It also needs early, consistent training. Sports activity helps it demonstrate its well-balanced disposition.

Health: PRA, HD.

Appropriate for: Beginners

QUICK INFO **FIC Group 1/No. 251:** *Sheepdogs and Cattle-dogs* **Country of Origin:** *Poland* **Size:** *males 18–20 inches (45–50 cm), females 16.5–18.5 inches (42–47 cm)* **Weight:** *approximately 33 pounds (15 kg)* **Fur:** *long, thick, shaggy, tends to tangle* **Color:** *all colors, including mottling (except for merle factor)* **Life Expectancy:** *12 years and longer*

Pomeranian

Also: *Miniature Spitz*

History: Even though this tiny dog comes from Pomerania, in Germany and Poland, it has been more popular in the United States and England than in Europe. In the 1960s it was reintroduced into Germany. Since that time it has been gaining more fans, even though it is not easy to breed.

Character: A happy, confident, intelligent dog with a boundless love for its master.

Living Conditions: A bit loud in its behavior as a watchdog. Self-assured to a fault—especially with bigger dogs. Otherwise, a good family dog.

Health: Displaced patella, cryptorchidism, hydrocephalus (water on the brain), PRA, heart and kidney diseases, tracheal collapse, epiphora, dwarfism, dystocia.

Appropriate for: Beginners

Training:	🐾🐾
City:	🐾
Family:	🐾🐾
Care:	🐾🐾🐾🐾🐾
Activity Level:	🐾🐾🐾

QUICK INFO **FIC Group 5/No. 97:** *Spitz and Primitive Types* **Country of Origin:** *Germany* **Size:** *9 inches (22 cm)* **Weight:** *4.4–6.6 pounds (2–3 kg)* **Fur:** *long, straight, erect topcoat that feels hard to the touch, with thick undercoat* **Color:** *black, white, brown, orange, spotty gray, crème, crème and sable, black and tan; spots: white background with evenly distributed spots* **Life Expectancy:** *approximately 15 years*

Pudelpointer

History: Fate ordained that a male standard poodle belonging to an officer taking part in maneuvers would mate with a brown female Pointer in a neighboring town. The result became the source of the Pudelpointers. This new breed was further developed under the supervision of Baron von Zedlitz, a hunting writer who used the pseudonym Hegewalt. Even though the Pudelpointer exceeds nearly all pointers in performance, unfortunately it is very rare.

Training: 🐾
City: no
Family: 🐾 🐾
Care: 🐾 🐾
Activity Level: 🐾 🐾 🐾 🐾 🐾

Character: This dog is trainable and spirited. It possesses natural toughness and an exceptional sense of smell. It learns very quickly and loves to retrieve. It's at home in the water.

Living Conditions: This dog is an outstanding housemate as long as it gets a chance to hunt. It can become a problem if it doesn't get adequate exercise.

Health: Rare hip dysplasia (HD).

Appropriate for: Hunters

QUICK INFO **FIC Group 7/No. 216:** *Pointers* **Country of Origin:** *Germany* **Size:** *males 24–27 inches (60–68 cm), females 22–25 inches (55–63 cm)* **Weight:** *55–77 pounds (25–35 kg)* **Fur:** *medium long, wiry, and hard* **Color:** *liver to dry leaf color* **Life Expectancy:** *12 to 14 years*

Pug (Mops)

History: The Pug became noticeable in Europe starting in the seventeenth century. Even since then it has been hopping and snuffling happily through our homes as an ideal indoor dog. Its fan club is constantly on the increase.

Training: 🐾🐾
City: 🐾
Family: 🐾
Care: 🐾🐾🐾
Activity Level: 🐾🐾🐾🐾

Character: This dog can be calm, and also very energetic and lively. Playful, friendly, and intelligent, it is easy to train.

Living Conditions: This dog does not smell or salivate. For a long time people thought it was lazy, dumb, and fat, but those opinions were quickly put to rest. With conscientious care, this dog is a champ.

Health: Jaw misalignment, inflammations and ulcerations of calluses, excessively long soft palate (snoring), tracheal collapse, dystocia, Legg-Perthes' disease, pattelar luxation.

Appropriate for: Beginners

QUICK INFO FIC Group 9/No. 253: *Companion and Toy Dogs* **Country of Origin:** *China (Great Britain)* **Size:** *10–12 inches (25–30 cm)* **Weight:** *14–18 pounds (6.3–8 kg)* **Fur:** *smooth, thick, shiny, soft* **Color:** *silver, apricot, light dun, black, black facemask; black stripe and black beauty marks on forehead and cheeks* **Life Expectancy:** *12 to 14 years*

Puli

History: There are people who believe that the Puli is the most intelligent dog in the world. In any case, it is surely the most versatile and, because of its external resemblance to the Komondor, one of the most unusual. It is presumed that this breed comes from dogs bred in India or Tibet.

Training:	🐾🐾
City:	🐾🐾🐾🐾🐾
Family:	🐾🐾
Care:	🐾🐾🐾🐾
Activity Level:	🐾🐾🐾🐾🐾

Character: This dog is active all day long and wants to herd everything that comes near it. It is also a very skillful watchdog. It needs close contact with its family.

Living Conditions: This dog is not a good choice for the city, since it needs lots of nature, wind, weather, and other animals. Anyone who wants to use it in substitute activities (dog sports or agility) will have to shear it, which shepherds do along with their sheep.

Health: Nothing is known about typical diseases.

Appropriate for: Experienced owners

QUICK INFO **FIC Group 1/No. 55:** *Sheepdogs and Cattledogs* **Country of Origin:** Hungary **Size:** *15.75–17 inches (40–43 cm)* **Weight:** *28.6–33 pounds (13–15 kg)* **Fur:** *long, thin strings and tangles covering the entire body* **Color:** *black with trace of rust or frost, white, gray, fawn, or fawn with a black mask* **Life Expectancy:** *over 15 years*

Pumi

History: When the Hungarians were importing Merino sheep because of their higher wool yield, strange herding dogs also came into the country and mixed with the native dogs. The Pumi gained recognition as a separate, versatile breed only at the beginning of the twentieth century. Today it is still common in Hungarian farmyards. It is scarcely known outside Hungary.

Training: 🐾
City: 🐾 🐾 🐾 🐾 🐾
Family: 🐾 🐾
Care: 🐾 🐾
Activity Level: 🐾 🐾 🐾 🐾 🐾

Character: This is a clever, adaptable working dog; it is attentive and watchful. It wants to be part of everything and be an active contributor.

Living Conditions: This very active work dog is not a good choice for inactive dog owners. Its fondness for barking also requires lots of patience. As a companion dog, it is good primarily for people who can devote plenty of free time to it.

Health: No known diseases in particular.

Appropriate for: Experienced owners

QUICK INFO **FIC Group 1/No. 56:** *Sheepdogs and Cattledogs* **Country of Origin:** *Hungary* **Size:** *13–17 inches (34–44 cm)* **Weight:** *17.5–29 pounds (8–13 kg)* **Fur:** *short, curly, with undercoat* **Color:** *white, black, gray, reddish brown* **Life Expectancy:** *12 to 14 years*

Pyrenean Mountain Dog

Also: *Great Pyrenees, Chien de Montagne des Pyrénées*

History: This is the largest of the familiar herding dogs. It protects the herds reliably in the Pyrenees Region. As early as the last century this hand-some dog was kept as a showpiece by nobles and bourgeois afficionados. Today this trend continues.

Character: This dog is friendly, affectionate, and calm only within its family. Since it is used to acting independently as a guardian of the herd, it needs careful and consistent training early on. Never use rigid discipline with this dog.

Living Conditions: It needs to live outdoors in all tempera-tures and lots of room both indoors and outdoors. Its fur requires care.

Health: HD, elbow dislocation, entropion, malocclusion, deafness, cataracts.

Appropriate for: Experienced owners

Training: 🐾 🐾 🐾
City: no
Family: 🐾 🐾 🐾
Care: 🐾 🐾 🐾 🐾
Activity Level: 🐾 🐾 🐾

QUICK INFO **FIC Group 2/No. 137:** *Pinschers, Schnauzers, Molossians, and Swiss Mountain and Cattledogs* **Country of Origin:** *France* **Size:** *males 27–32 inches (68.5–81 cm), females 25–29 inches (63.5–74 cm)* **Weight:** *88–123 pounds (40–56 kg)* **Fur:** *double, very thin, long or half long, a bit longer on throat, tail, and trousers* **Color:** *white* **Life Expectancy:** *up to 15 years*

187

Rhodesian Ridgeback

History: This dog's name refers to a stripe along the spine where the hairs grow in the opposite direction. This was the dog of the Hottentots in Africa. The white settlers refined its appearance by crossing it with Airedale Terriers, Collies, and Bloodhounds. Later on it was used for hunting lions; it would corner the lion so that the hunter could shoot it.

Training: 🐾🐾
City: no
Family: 🐾
Care: 🐾
Activity Level: 🐾🐾🐾🐾🐾

Character: Intelligent, adaptable, powerful, and spirited. It needs careful and gentle, consistent training, for this late developer can also be sensitive.

Living Conditions: One mustn't forget that this is a hunting dog that needs lots of exercise to replace the hunt. This is an ideal dog for active people who understand dogs well.

Health: Dermoid sinus (the canal over and/or under the ridge that follows the direction of the spinal column), HD, hypothyroidism, deafness.

Appropriate for: Experienced owners

QUICK INFO FIC Group 6/No. 146: *Scent Hounds and Related Breeds* **Country of Origin:** *South Africa* **Size:** *24–27 inches (61–69 cm)* **Weight:** *64–75 pounds (29–34 kg)* **Fur:** *short, thick, smooth, shiny* **Color:** *wheat yellow to fox red* **Life Expectancy:** *12 to 14 years*

Rottweiler

History: This herding dog from Rottweil in Schwaben, Germany, helped butchers by driving their cattle into the slaughterhouse, then pulling the butchers' cart when delivering meat. In recent times, unfortunately, some unscrupulous breeders used the most aggressive Rottweilers in the gene pool and this nearly ruined the breed.

Training: 🐾
City: 🐾 🐾 🐾 🐾
Family: 🐾
Care: 🐾
Activity Level: 🐾 🐾 🐾 🐾 🐾

Character: Dogs from conscientious breeders are steadfast, devoted, and ready to partake of work and training. They are devoted and willing and will focus on the handler quite well.

Living Conditions: This dog thrives on training and requires a significant amount of leadership instruction and socialization that must be continued for life.

Health: HD, heart problems, circulatory weakness under stress, crucial ligament tears, entropion, ectropion, elbow dysplasia, diabetes.

Appropriate for: Experienced owners

QUICK INFO FIC Group 2/No. 147: *Pinschers, Schnauzers, Molossians, and Swiss Mountain and Cattledogs* **Country of Origin:** *Germany* **Size:** *males 24–26.75 inches (62–68 cm), females 22–25 inches (56–63 cm)* **Weight:** *92–110 pounds (42–50 kg)* **Fur:** *tough, tight to body* **Color:** *black with reddish-brown markings* **Life Expectancy:** *over 10 years*

Saarloos Wolfhound

Also: *Saarloos Wolfdog*

History: At the start of the twentieth century, a ship's cook named Leendert Saarloos, who was a dog fanatic, wanted to cross his German Shepherd and a female wolf to create a breed that had all the physical and psychological qualities of the wolf.

Character: This questionable experiment produced dogs in which wolf behavior is still clearly visible. Very distrustful and cautious with all strangers. Wolfdogs are very intelligent, and have more acute senses and better reactive abilities than most dogs.

Living Conditions: The Saarloos needs absolutely secure quarters; in addition the owner needs to have lots of knowledge of wolves and their ownership.

Health: No particular known diseases.

Appropriate for: Very few specialists

Training: 🐾 🐾 🐾
City: no
Family: 🐾 🐾 🐾 🐾
Care: 🐾
Activity Level: 🐾 🐾 🐾 🐾 🐾

QUICK INFO **FIC Group 1/No. 311:** *Sheepdogs and Cattledogs* **Country of Origin:** *Netherlands* **Size:** *25.5–27.5 inches (65–70 cm)* **Weight:** *66–88 pounds (30–40 kg)* **Fur:** *short hair with undercoat, shorter and smoother than on a wolf* **Color:** *brown and wolf colors on a gray background, light cream colors to white* **Life Expectancy:** *12 to 14 years*

Saint Bernard

History: The Saint Bernard became famous as a dog that could rescue people lost in the snow, acting on its own impulse. Formerly Saint Bernards were at least a third smaller and weighed less than half of today's giants.

Training: 🐾🐾
City: no
Family: 🐾
Care: 🐾🐾🐾
Activity Level: 🐾🐾🐾

Character: Good natured, obedient, and very loyal, patient with children. It also has adequate guarding instinct, which it can apply enthusiastically when needed.

Living Conditions: It needs close bonding with its master and hates confinement to a kennel. Has no great need to run, so it must be exercised reasonably. Gradually, breeders are working to improve the gene pool of these dogs.

Health: HD is still to common in this breed, other skeletal problems, eye problems, cysts on salivary glands, diabetes, gastric torsion, bone cancer.

Appropriate for: Experienced owners

QUICK INFO FIC Group 2/No. 61: *Pinschers, Schnauzers, Molossians, and Swiss Mountain and Cattledogs* **Country of Origin:** *Switzerland* **Size:** *males 27–35 inches (70–90 cm), females 27–31 inches (65–80 cm)* **Weight:** *up to 175 pounds (80 kg)* **Fur:** *long and short hair* **Color:** *white with reddish-brown blotches, dark markings on head* **Life Expectancy:** *8 to 10 years*

Saluki

Also: *Tazi*

History: Evidently today's form of the Saluki has existed for thousands of years all over the Orient. It came to England with Arabian horses around 1700, and from there it spread through continental Europe.

Training:	🐾 🐾 🐾
City:	no
Family:	🐾 🐾 🐾
Care:	🐾
Activity Level:	🐾 🐾 🐾 🐾 🐾

Character: A very quiet and distinguished appearing dog, which forms a close bond with its master. Tends to be shy around children. This dog is fairly stubborn and strong willed. In addition, it is sensitive, often very anxious and easily frightened.

Living Conditions: This swift dog needs lots of exercise, and that involves considerable expense in special racing clubs. Obedience training can make this dog feel a bit more secure.

Health: Illnesses involving skin and the digestive system, for example, can result from stress, PRA, retinal detachment.

Appropriate for: Experienced owners

QUICK INFO **FIC Group 10/No. 269:** *Sighthounds*
Country of Origin: *Middle East* **Size:** *23–28 inches (58.5–71 cm)* **Weight:** *29–66 pounds (13–30 kg)* **Fur:** *smooth, silky, with or without feathers on the legs and the underside of the tail* **Color:** *all colors and color combinations are permissible*
Life Expectancy: *13 to 16 years*

Samoyed

Also: *Samoiedskaya Sabaka*

History: According to eighteenth-century travelers' accounts, the Samoyeds, a tribe in northern Russia, used white Spitzes for hunting, pulling sleds, and herding reindeer. In precarious situations, the explorer Raould Amundsen always relied on this dog's survival instinct.

Character: Samoyeds are not as aggressive toward other dogs as other sled dog breeds. They are gentle, and they like people, especially children. Obedient and devoted, they need close contact with people.

Living Conditions: Samoyeds like to be kept busy and need lots of exercise. This confident dog needs consistent and gentle training.

Health: HD, deafness, PRA, diabetes, dwarfism.

Appropriate for: Beginners

Training: 🐾 🐾 🐾
City: 🐾 🐾 🐾 🐾 🐾
Family: 🐾
Care: 🐾 🐾 🐾 🐾 🐾
Activity Level: 🐾 🐾 🐾 🐾

QUICK INFO **FIC Group 5/No. 212:** *Spitz and Primitive Types* **Country of Origin:** *Russia* **Size:** *20–22 inches (50–55 cm)* **Weight:** *44–66 pounds (20–30 kg)* **Fur:** *soft, medium long with thick, woolly undercoat and fairly hard, weatherproof top coat* **Color:** *white, cream colored* **Life Expectancy:** *over 10 years*

Sarplaninac

**Also: *Yugoslavian Sheepdog,
Yugoslavian Mountain Dog*
Formerly: *Illyrian Shepherd***

Training: 🐾 🐾 🐾
City: no
Family: 🐾 🐾 🐾
Care: 🐾 🐾 🐾
Activity Level: 🐾 🐾 🐾

History: This dog's duties have always involved watching and protecting the herds independently. In town it defended house and home. In Yugoslavia it is bred for military and police work because of its toughness.

Character: This is a serious, independent dog. It is a positively faithful and devoted guardian of its family. In spite of consistent training, it is never a totally obedient dog.

Living Conditions: It needs a fenced yard away from all other dogs, where it doesn't need to spend the whole day under watchdog stress. It enjoys outdoor excursions involving the family.

Health: HD.

Appropriate for: Specialists

QUICK INFO FIC Group 2/No. 41: *Pinschers, Schnauzers, Molossians, and Swiss Mountain and Cattledogs* **Country of Origin:** *Macedonia/Yugoslavia* **Size:** *males at least 24 inches (62 cm), females at least 23 inches (58 cm)* **Weight:** *males, 77–99 pounds (35–45 kg); females, 66–88 pounds (30–40 kg)* **Fur:** *long, thick, hard with fairly thick undercoat* **Color:** *all white to black, preferred steel gray and dark gray* **Life Expectancy:** *10 to 12 years*

Schapendoes

Also: *Dutch Sheepdog, Dutch Sheep Poodle*

Training:	🐾
City:	🐾 🐾 🐾 🐾
Family:	🐾
Care:	🐾 🐾 🐾
Activity Level:	🐾 🐾 🐾 🐾 🐾

History: The Schapendoes (which means *sheep poodle*), the former herding dog of the heathland, had been nearly forgotten in Holland and was saved as a breed only in 1940 when the Dutch herding breeds were cataloged. The present day breed was created from survivors with the help of experienced breeders and geneticists. The breed gained recognition in 1968.

Character: A friendly, playful, lively family dog. It is watchful, but not vicious. Indoors it is calm and not nervous. In training it you need to use patience and consistency, for as a herding dog it is accustomed to acting independently.

Living Conditions: Because of its work ethic and temperament, it needs adequate activity in dog competitions and agility.

Health: No particular known illnesses.

Appropriate for: Beginners

QUICK INFO FIC Group 1/No. 313: *Sheepdogs and Cattle-dogs* **Country of Origin:** *the Netherlands* **Size:** *16–20 inches (40–50 cm)* **Weight:** *approximately 33 pounds (15 kg)* **Fur:** *medium long, shaggy, with undercoat* **Color:** *all colors permissible* **Life Expectancy:** *over 10 years*

Schipperke

History: Cynologists are not in agreement about whether the Schipperke is a Spitz or a Shepherd. From an anatomical viewpoint, it is a Spitz. In translation, the Flemish word *scheperke* means *small shepherd dog*. Today the word *Schipperke* generally is interpreted as designating a *Ship Spitz*, because this dog is often used on ships and barges as a watchdog, and as a ratter and mouser in homes.

Training: 🐾
City: 🐾 🐾
Family: 🐾
Care: 🐾
Activity Level: 🐾 🐾 🐾

Character: This is a cheerful, lively, alert dog that is very patient with the children in the family. It is watchful and likes to bark. Very quick to learn and devoted. It doesn't like strangers.

Living Conditions: Because of its healthy daintiness and adaptability, it is an ideal dog for indoors, if you can tolerate its barking.

Health: Entropion, Legg-Perthes' disease, hypothyroidism.

Appropriate for: Beginners

QUICK INFO FIC Group 1 /No. 83: *Sheepdogs and Cattledogs* **Country of Origin:** *Belgium* **Size:** *9–13 inches (22–33 cm)* **Weight:** *6.6–17.6 pounds (3–8 kg)* **Fur:** *abundant, thick, and hard; sticks out because of undercoat; has a ruff* **Color:** *black* **Life Expectancy:** *over 15 years*

Schnauzer

History: Originally this dog was the hairy brother of the Pinscher (see page 178), with which it hunted rats and mice in southern German farmyards and in city horse stables. In 1882, Max Hartenstein began breeding Schnauzers. Its brother entered the breed list as the German Pinscher.

Training: 🐾 🐾
City: 🐾
Family: 🐾
Care: 🐾 🐾 🐾 🐾
Activity Level: 🐾 🐾 🐾

Character: The Schnauzer has remained an earthy dog that needs close bonding with its family. It is spirited, alert, quick to learn, and fearless. Always watchful and ready to defend, but not vicious.

Living Conditions: This dog needs regular exercise, preferably in dog sports. Its training must be consistent and gentle. With appropriate socializing and good obedience training, even its scrappiness can be kept under control.

Health: PRA, heart problems, cataracts, von Willebrand's disease, Legg-Perthes' disease, microphthalmus.

Appropriate for: Beginners

QUICK INFO FIC Group 2/No. 182: *Pinschers and Schnauzers, Molossians, and Swiss Mountain and Cattledogs* **Country of Origin:** *Germany* **Size:** *18–20 inches (45–50 cm)* **Weight:** *33 pounds (15 kg)* **Fur:** *hard, rough, with thick undercoat* **Color:** *black, salt and pepper* **Life Expectancy:** *over 15 years*

Scottish Terrier

History: Once a short-legged Scottish hunting Terrier used for hunting predatory game, recently this dog has made a career as a stylish companion dog. West Highland White, Cairn, and Sky Terriers had a hand in its origin. In the 1930s the Scottish Terrier, along with the Fox Terrier, was highly fashionable. At first this dog was also referred to as the Aberdeen Terrier and was very popular for many years.

Training: 🐾 🐾 🐾
City: 🐾
Family: 🐾
Care: 🐾 🐾 🐾 🐾 🐾
Activity Level: 🐾 🐾 🐾

Character: This dog makes a grumpy, morose impression. This impression is further confirmed, for it is shy around strangers. This is a brave, independent, and strong willed Terrier with a big personality.

Living Conditions: This dog requires careful and consistent training and control. Absolute obedience is not an attainable goal. It doesn't need a tremendous amount of exercise.

Health: Scottie cramp (a walking disorder), epilepsy, eczema, von Willebrand's disease, deafness, urinary calculi.

Appropriate for: Beginners

QUICK INFO FIC Group 3/No. 73: Terriers **Country of Origin:** Scotland **Size:** 10–11 inches (25–28 cm) **Weight:** 19–23 pounds (8.6–10.4 kg) **Fur:** hard, thick, rough, with soft undercoat; regular trimming needed **Color:** black, wheat, striped **Life Expectancy:** 12 to more than 15 years

Sealyham Terrier

History: The Dandie Dinmont Terrier, West Highland White Terrier, Welsh Corgi, and White Bull Terrier contributed to the origin of this dog. This was a tough dog on badger hunts and was carefully selected for performance.

Training: 🐾 🐾 🐾
City: 🐾
Family: 🐾
Care: 🐾 🐾 🐾 🐾
Activity Level: 🐾 🐾 🐾

Character: This is a happy, playful, pleasant housedog. It is friendly, fearless, and resolute. This is a blend of a good watchdog and a big voice. It is reserved with strangers.

Living Conditions: This dog likes hunting activities, so it needs to be kept occupied. Consistent training requires a little patience. The Sealyham Terrier takes shameless advantage of any weaknesses in its trainer.

Health: Skin diseases, deafness, eczema, dystocia, lens luxation.

Appropriate for: Beginners

QUICK INFO FIC Group 3/No. 74: *Terriers* **Country of Origin:** *Great Britain* **Size:** *maximum 12.25 inches (31 cm)* **Weight:** *17.6–22 pounds (8–10 kg)* **Fur:** *hard, long top coat with soft undercoat; needs regular trimming* **Color:** *pure white, colored markings on head permissible* **Life Expectancy:** *12 years or longer*

Shar-pei

History: A rare Chinese dog breed; it always causes a sensation and stimulates discussion because of its wrinkled appearance. The origins of this dog are unknown. Puppies are wrinkled all over, adults have fewer wrinkles. This breed would practically have ceased to exist even in China if it hadn't been marketed intensively in the United States.

Training: 🐾 🐾 🐾
City: 🐾
Family: 🐾 🐾 🐾
Care: 🐾 🐾
Activity Level: 🐾 🐾 🐾

Character: The Shar-pei is very strong willed and has a serious, dignified character. When it wants, it can also be comical and tender.

Living Conditions: This dog must be kept indoors in close association with the family. It hates water and the cold. It needs consistent training and strict management.

Health: Skin problems, eyelid abnormalities, HD, general skeletal problems, photophobia.

Appropriate for: Experienced owners

QUICK INFO FIC Group 2/No. 309: *Pinschers and Schnauzers, Molossians, and Swiss Mountain and Cattledogs* **Country of Origin:** *China* **Size:** *18–20 inches (45–50 cm)* **Weight:** *44–55 pounds (20–25 kg)* **Fur:** *short, hard* **Color:** *all black, russet, cream* **Life Expectancy:** *8 to 10 years*

Shetland Sheepdog

Also: *Sheltie*

History: The Sheltie is not simply a small Collie, but rather a mixture of a small Shetland farm dog and Dwarf Spaniel, Papillon, and Dwarf Spitz. It originated on the Shetland Islands and is more popular than the Collie in the United States. In other countries this dog is comparatively rare.

Character: Very spirited and clever but nervous around strangers and tiny children. It tends to be quite verbal and this should be subdued by gentle training.

Living Conditions: Gentleness is required for this very sensitive but easily trained dog. Yelling will always be counterproductive, especially when training. Shelties are an excellent choice for competitive dog sports and agility trials.

Health: Epilepsy, deafness associated with blue merle (see page 18), heart diseases, ectasia, von Willebrand's disease, HD, nasal solar dermatitis, cataracts, PRA, hypothyroidism, and others.

Appropriate for: Beginners

Training: 🐾 🐾
City: 🐾
Family: 🐾
Care: 🐾 🐾 🐾 🐾
Activity Level: 🐾 🐾 🐾 🐾

QUICK INFO FIC Group 1/No. 88: *Sheepdogs and Cattledogs* **Country of Origin:** *Great Britain* **Size:** *14–14.5 inches (35–37 cm)* **Weight:** *13.2–15 pounds (6–7 kg)* **Fur:** *long, hard topcoat with soft undercoat* **Color:** *sable, tricolor, blue merle, black, black with various white portions* **Life Expectancy:** *10 to 15 years*

Shiba Inu

History: This dog is one of the old Japanese Spitzes, which have existed in Japan for many years, according to depictions and sculptures. Evidently it was used for hunting birds and other wild game, for its name means *little bush dog*. It is currently being bred in the United States.

Training: 🐾🐾🐾
City: 🐾
Family: 🐾🐾
Care: 🐾🐾🐾
Activity Level: 🐾🐾🐾🐾🐾

Character: The Shiba is intelligent and confident. Lively and enterprising, but it never plays second fiddle. It is an eager learner, but only with the person that it respects.

Living Conditions: This is another very primitive dog, so it requires a certain amount of knowledge on the owner's part. Its passion for hunting means that it can't be allowed to run free. It likes to be outdoors, but wants close bonding with people. It needs lots of activity.

Health: HD, PRA, patellar luxation.

Appropriate for: Experienced owners

QUICK INFO FIC Group 5/No. 257: *Spitz and Primitive Types* **Country of Origin:** *Japan* **Size:** *males 15.5 inches (39.5 cm), females 14.5 inches (36.5 cm)* **Weight:** *22–29 pounds (10–13 kg)* **Fur:** *double, with soft, thick undercoat and harsh, straight guard hairs* **Color:** *red, black and tan, sesame, black and sesame, red and sesame* **Life Expectancy:** *12 to 15 years*

Shih Tzu

History: This dog is one of the far-eastern lion dogs that supposedly guarded the Buddhist temples and were given as gifts to the highest-ranking individuals. That's how the Shi-Tze-kou (the Tibetan Lion Dog) was brought to the imperial palace in China, where it was developed into the Shih Tzu.

Training: 🐾🐾🐾
City: 🐾
Family: 🐾🐾
Care: 🐾🐾🐾🐾🐾
Activity Level: 🐾🐾🐾

Character: This dog is very spirited and has a friendly disposition. It is a loving, playful, and confident dog that is a perfect companion for people who aren't put off by endless grooming, or the dog can be sheared.

Living Conditions: This dog is not particularly fond of the summer heat and does not tolerate it well. Its only demand is to be loved, and it returns that love.

Health: Kneecap dislocation, breathing difficulties, cleft palate, entropion, ectropion, kidney diseases, ear infections, eye problems such as corneal ulcers.

Appropriate for: Beginners

QUICK INFO FIC Group 9/No. 208: *Companion and Toy dogs* **Country of Origin:** *Tibet* **Size:** *approximately 11 inches (27 cm)* **Weight:** *approximately 20 pounds (9 kg)* **Fur:** *long, thick, with short, thick undercoat* **Color:** *all colors* **Life Expectancy:** *approximately 10 years*

Siberian Husky

History: This is one of the Nordic dogs that is not very common in many areas. Its passion is to be harnessed to a sled as part of a team and pull it through the falling snow. The Husky comes from Siberia and reached us by way of Alaska.

Training: 🐾 🐾 🐾
City: no
Family: 🐾 🐾 🐾
Care: 🐾 🐾
Activity Level: 🐾 🐾 🐾 🐾 🐾

Character: This dog is loving and even-tempered with its family, and friendly with strangers. It learns quickly, but doesn't obey reliably. It has a strong drive for hunting and adventure.

Living Conditions: The yard has to be breakout proof. This breed absolutely needs activity and a chance to run: wagon and sled races, running alongside a bicycle, and jogging—and every day!

Health: HD, PRA, skin diseases, epilepsy, von Willebrand's disease, glaucoma.

Appropriate for: Experienced owners

QUICK INFO FIC Group 5/No. 270: *Spitz and Primitive Types* **Country of Origin:** *United States* **Size:** *males 21–24 inches (53–60 cm), females 20–22 inches (51–56 cm)* **Weight:** *35–59 pounds (16–27 kg)* **Fur:** *thick, double, woolly* **Color:** *all colors and shades* **Life Expectancy:** *10 years and longer*

Skye Terrier

History: Evidently this is the oldest Scottish terrier. It comes from the Isle of Skye in northwestern Scotland, and it was very popular in the Scottish and English courts. It was tough and effective against vermin, but for a long time it has been bred as a show dog. An interesting fact: it is four times longer than high, and yet it has none of the connective tissue problems that plague the Dachshund.

Training: 🐾🐾🐾
City: 🐾
Family: 🐾🐾🐾
Care: 🐾🐾🐾🐾🐾
Activity Level: 🐾🐾🐾

Character: This dog is a typical Terrier that loves to dig and follow its prey underground. It has great stamina and courage and is quite agile in the bargain. It is an affectionate, loyal, and happy character with its family but is reserved and cautious with strangers. It is fine with well-mannered children and very reserved with loud and boisterous kids.

Living Conditions: It thrives on kind, consistent training and likes long walks with its handler.

Health: Tracheal collapse, patellar luxation, Legg-Perthes' disease, diabetes, cardiovascular abnormalities.

Appropriate for: Experienced owners

QUICK INFO **FIC Group 3/No. 75:** *Terriers* **Country of Origin:** *Great Britain* **Size:** *10 inches (25 cm)* **Weight:** *25 pounds (11.5 kg)* **Fur:** *long, heavy, straight, with soft undercoat* **Color:** *gray, tan, cream with black markings on ears and muzzle* **Life Expectancy:** *approximately 10 to 12 years*

Sloughi

Also: *Arabian Greyhound*

History: We know from depictions in Egyptian reliefs that the ancient Egyptians used similar greyhounds for hunting as early as 1500 B.C. The Bedouins brought Sloughis on the hunt and held them in front of them on the saddle; when the dog spotted the game, it leaped from the horse, chased the game, and cornered it. Today the dogs still live as spoiled, prized possessions inside the tents.

Character: This dog is gentle, adaptable, and friendly yet reserved with its people. This is no dog for people who expect slavish obedience from it.

Living Conditions: This dog can live only with close family bonding. It needs lots of exercise, and especially, contact with its humans. It is most comfortable in calm surroundings.

Health: No particular illnesses.

Appropriate for: Experienced owners

Training: 🐾 🐾 🐾
City: no
Family: 🐾 🐾
Care: 🐾
Activity Level: 🐾 🐾 🐾 🐾 🐾

QUICK INFO FIC Group 10/No. 188: *Sighthounds* **Country of Origin:** *Morocco* **Size:** *males 26–28 inches (66–72 cm), females 24–27 inches (61–68 cm)* **Weight:** *44–59 pounds (20–27 kg)* **Fur:** *short, thick, and fine* **Color:** *all shades of sandy colors (also with mask, striping, etc.) are permissible* **Life Expectancy:** *12 years*

Small Munsterlander

History: Unfortunately, because of a television series, commercial vendors have become aware of this breed, so that when you buy one you have to be careful you don't get a genetically impaired, unpedigreed dog from a hobby breeder. This is the smallest of the German pointers, and it is a descendent of the bird dogs of the Middle Ages.

Training: 🐾
City: 🐾 🐾 🐾 🐾
Family: 🐾
Care: 🐾 🐾
Activity Level: 🐾 🐾 🐾 🐾 🐾

Character: Lively and devoted, good with children and other house pets. It is very quick to learn and is very obedient with gentle, consistent training. It is watchful but not nippy.

Living Conditions: This handsome, intelligent, and versatile hunting dog belongs in the family of a hunter.

Health: Rare HD, entropion.

Appropriate for: Beginners, hunters

QUICK INFO FIC Group 7/No. 102: *Pointers* **Country of Origin:** *Germany* **Size:** *20–22 inches (50–56 cm)* **Weight:** *approximately 33 pounds (15 kg)* **Fur:** *medium long, plain, close, with feathers on tail; forelegs feathered, trousers on hind legs* **Color:** *white and brown with blotches or jacket, gray* **Life Expectancy:** *10 to 12 years*

Spitz

Also: *Pomeranian*

History: The Spitz is the oldest form of housedog and goes back to the Stone Age, to the peat dogs and the later pile village Spitz. In the Middle Ages it was the most common farm dog. In contrast to the Nordic Spitz, it couldn't be trained to hunt, so feudal lords allowed the farmers to own this type of dog.

The fairly common Medium Spitz performed reliable duty as a herding dog and kept the farmyard free of rats and mice; the Great and Small Spitz were kept mostly as companion dogs. In town, the Medium Spitz was also frequently seen herding the geese and even the cattle. Queen Victoria kept several small Spitzes or Pomeranians. It is present in literature as the classic watchdog. Unfortunately, the German Spitz has not been very popular for several decades, and it's a shame that such an old and beautiful dog breed no longer attracts so much attention. The decline of this beautiful breed is perhaps due to the intensive care required, which still doesn't keep the fur from becoming tangled. Since the Spitz is also difficult to train, and very loud because of its tremendous watchfulness, some dog owners are scared away from getting a Spitz.

Character: This dog is intelligent and quick to learn, confident, and not immediately submissive. As a territorial, watchful dog that likes to bark, it is distrustful of strangers. The Spitz is devoted to its family, and it has lots of patience with

children. It tends to be critical of other dogs.

Training: 🐾 🐾 🐾 🐾
City: 🐾 🐾 🐾 🐾
Family: 🐾
Care: 🐾 🐾 🐾 🐾
Activity Level: 🐾 🐾 🐾

Living Conditions: Since this dog doesn't roam and is loyal to its home, there is no problem with keeping this robust and storm proof dog outdoors. It also doesn't need to be taken for regular walks. It's much happier when it can watch everything in the yard. The Spitz usually prefers country life because of its ancient habits.

Health: No common diseases.

Appropriate for: Beginners

QUICK INFO **FIC Group 5/No. 97:** *Spitz and Primitive Types* **Country of Origin:** *Germany* **Size:** *large Spitz (page 208): 16–20 inches (40–50 cm); medium Spitz (above, left): 11.5–14 inches (29–36 cm); small Spitz (top right): 9–11 inches (23–28 cm)* **Weight:** *large Spitz: 55 pounds (25 kg); medium Spitz: 13.2–15.4 pounds (6–7 kg); small Spitz: 8.8–10.2 pounds (4–5 kg)* **Fur:** *abundant all over body, short on muzzle, ears, and paws* **Color:** *large and medium Spitz: black, white, brown; small Spitz: the foregoing, plus orange and wolf colors* **Life Expectancy:** *large Spitz: 12 to 13 years; medium Spitz: 13 to 15 years; small Spitz: 14 to 15 years*

Staffordshire Bull Terrier

History: At the start of the nineteenth century, many Britons delighted in animal fights or bet on which dog could kill the most rats in a certain period of time. Later on the dogs were allowed to fight against each

Training: 🐾🐾
City: 🐾🐾🐾🐾
Family: 🐾🐾🐾
Care: 🐾
Activity Level: 🐾🐾🐾

other. For this purpose the "Staff" was produced from a mixture of local Terriers and English Bulldogs. These dogs were trained to fight to the death with anything that looked like a dog.

Character: This dog is friendly, lovable, and very devoted to people. As a dominant dog, it needs early and continued training and socialization with other dogs.

Living Conditions: Even with the best trained "Staffs," their scrappiness sometimes breaks through.

Health: Skin diseases, as well as kidney stones and eye problems.

Note: In some places, such as throughout Germany, it is against the law to own or breed this dog.

QUICK INFO FIC Group 3/No. 76: *Terriers* **Country of Origin:** *Great Britain* **Size:** *14–16 inches (36–41 cm)* **Weight:** *24–37.4 pounds (11–17 kg)* **Fur:** *short, smooth, close* **Color:** *all colors except black and tan, and liver* **Life Expectancy:** *12 to 14 years*

Standard Poodle

Also: *King Poodle*

History: A very old hunting dog whose origin is still not well known. In any case, the Poodle was an outstanding hunting dog especially for waterfowling. It was the basis for many hunting and guard dogs. It is bred in four size categories. The poodle is one of the most beloved companion dogs of our time, despite its particular clipping, which is intended mainly for dog shows.

Character: Poodles can learn anything. They are easy to train, sociable, receptive, and merry playmates with well-mannered children. They are watchful but not vicious.

Living Conditions: This is a robust dog that loves to run and always wants to be part of things. It needs close bonding with the family and is well suited for dog sports (dog competitions and agility). Poodles don't shed.

Health: HD, ear infections, eye problems, PRA, and others.

Appropriate for: Beginners

Training:	🐾
City:	🐾
Family:	🐾
Care:	🐾 🐾 🐾 🐾 🐾
Activity Level:	🐾 🐾 🐾 🐾

QUICK INFO **FIC Group 9/No. 172:** *Companion and Toy Dogs* **Size:** *18–23 inches (45–58 cm)* **Weight:** *48 pounds (22 kg)* **Fur:** *double, abundant, woolly, and curly* **Color:** *black, white, chestnut brown, silver, and apricot* **Life Expectancy:** *10 to 14 years*

211

Sussex Spaniel

History: This dog was bred in the county of Sussex as a hunting dog for the thick undergrowth. It was intended for slow, deliberate searching. Despite its outstanding sense of smell, the breed never really caught on, and it is rare even in its homeland.

Training: 🐾 🐾
City: 🐾 🐾 🐾
Family: 🐾 🐾
Care: 🐾 🐾 🐾
Activity Level: 🐾 🐾 🐾

Character: This dog radiates friendliness and kindness in part because of its hazelnut-brown eyes. It forms a close bond with its person, but outdoors it shows an appropriate amount of enthusiasm for the hunt. This dog is easily controllable and quick to learn.

Living Conditions: Since this is a hunting dog, it shouldn't run free. It likes to go for walks with its handler, but they mustn't be too long. It enjoys alternative activities when it can't go hunting.

Health: No particular diseases.

Appropriate for: Beginners

QUICK INFO FIC Group 8/No. 127: *Retrievers, Flushing Dogs, and Water Dogs* **Country of Origin:** *Great Britain* **Size:** *15–16 inches (38–41 cm)* **Weight:** *approximately 51 pounds (23 kg)* **Fur:** *abundant, smooth with thick, waterproof undercoat* **Color:** *golden-liver color with golden hair tips* **Life Expectancy:** *up to 15 years*

Tervuren

Also: *Belgian Tervuren*

History: This is surely the most versa-tile of the four Belgian shepherd breeds. Fans of the Tervuren even feel that it has the same qualities as the highly regarded German Shepherd (see page 112).

Training: 🐾
City: 🐾 🐾 🐾
Family: 🐾 🐾
Care: 🐾 🐾 🐾
Activity Level: 🐾 🐾 🐾 🐾

Character: This dog is intelligent, and it learns quickly. It may also be a little nervous and sensitive. It doesn't tolerate harsh commands, and it is easily controllable. It is affectionate and loving in the family, including with well-mannered children.

Living Conditions: This dog prefers to be active and kept busy. It is a good dog for competitive dog sports and agility. If the dog is trained as a guard dog, people should avoid irritating it. In recent years the Tervuren has proved its worth as a seeing-eye dog and an aid to the handicapped.

Health: Cramp-like attacks, hypothyroidism, epilepsy, pancreatic disorders.

Appropriate for: Beginners

QUICK INFO FIC Group 1/No. 15: *Sheepdogs and Cattle-dogs* **Country of Origin:** *Belgium* **Size:** *22–26 inches (55–66 cm)* **Weight:** *60–63 pounds (27.5–28.5 kg)* **Fur:** *long, smooth, double* **Color:** *mahogany to beige, gray with black mask and long, coarse black hairs* **Life Expectancy:** *12 to 14 years*

Tibetan Spaniel

History: This is another of the lion dogs that were trained to turn the prayer wheels in Tibetan monasteries. In the winter the monks would carry them like living hot-water bottles. This dog has a bit more nose than the other temple dogs, so it doesn't attract as much attention, perhaps because it doesn't have to struggle so much to take in air.

Training:	🐾🐾
City:	🐾
Family:	🐾
Care:	🐾🐾🐾
Activity Level:	🐾🐾🐾

Character: This is an active, robust, tough little imp. As a temple watchdog, it has an aversion to strangers. It likes action and runs and tumbles with the children as hard as it can. It allows itself to be trained, as long as you are more resolute than the dog.

Living Conditions: It has modest demands, including in regard to exercise. Above all, it must be kept from excessive heat.

Health: PRA, kidney problems.

Appropriate for: Beginners

QUICK INFO FIC Group 9/No. 231: *Companion and Toy Dogs* **Country of Origin:** *Tibet* **Size:** *approximately 10 inches (25 cm)* **Weight:** *9–15 pounds (4.1–6.8 kg)* **Fur:** *moderately long, silky, double, well feathered on legs and ears* **Color:** *all colors and combinations* **Life Expectancy:** *13 to 14 years*

Tibetan Terrier

History: The Tibetan Terrier has as little to do with Terriers as the Tibetan Spaniel (see page 214) has to do with Spaniels. Originally this dog was a cattle herder for Tibetan farmers in the toughest conditions at an altitude of

Training: 🐾 🐾
City: 🐾 🐾
Family: 🐾
Care: 🐾 🐾 🐾
Activity Level: 🐾 🐾 🐾 🐾

15,500 feet (3000 m). Supposedly it was crossed with a Hungarian Puli after 1920, probably to make its fur a little softer.
Character: Active, fond of running and jumping. Good natured and playful in the family. In spite of its possible inflexibility, it can be trained with kindness and patience. Its reserve with strangers is often considered a character weakness.
Living Conditions: This dog doesn't like being alone because it is very attached. It needs adequate activity to stimulate its mind as well as its athletic body. Competitive dog sports and agility are good choices as long as the dog has no problems with HD.
Health: HD, hypothyroidism, PRA, anesthesia sensitivity.
Appropriate for: Beginners

QUICK INFO *FIC Group 9/No. 209: Companion and Toy Dogs* **Country of Origin:** *Tibet* **Size:** *14–16 inches (35–41 cm)* **Weight:** *17.5–31 pounds (8–14 kg)* **Fur:** *long, abundant, straight or wavy, never curly, with thick undercoat* **Color:** *all except chocolate* **Life Expectancy:** *13 to 14 years*

Tiroler Bracke

History: This breed is slightly smaller and lighter than the Brandlbracke (see page 67). This is an outstanding scent hound in the high mountains. Its hereditary skills are its reliability on track and trail, its ability to locate

Training: 🐾
City: no
Family: 🐾 🐾
Care: 🐾
Activity Level: 🐾 🐾 🐾 🐾 🐾

downed game, and signaling the find by barking. The Tiroler Bracke is used for hunting more than rabbits and foxes. It vociferously follows a hot trail. Outside of Germany and Austria, it is practically unknown.

Character: A very desirable hunting dog that also fits in well with the family and behaves lovingly. It is peaceable and well balanced when it has a chance to go hunting.

Living Conditions: These dogs do best in a hunting family because the Tiroler Bracke may become melancholy without hunting activity.

Health: No particular known illnesses.

Appropriate for: Hunters

QUICK INFO FIC Group 6/No. 68: *Scent Hounds and Related Breeds* **Country of Origin:** *Austria* **Size:** *16.5–20 inches (42–50 cm)* **Weight:** *40–44 pounds (18–20 kg)* **Fur:** *short, smooth, close* **Color:** *red, black and red, tricolor* **Life Expectancy:** *12 to 14 years*

Toy Poodle

History: With dog breeds, the designation *toy* means that the dog is even
smaller than the breed's miniature
form. Against the recommendation
of eleven member countries of the
FCI, the French pushed through
recognition of the Toy Poodle as a breed.

Training:	🐾
City:	🐾
Family:	🐾🐾🐾
Care:	🐾🐾🐾🐾🐾
Activity Level:	🐾🐾🐾

Character/Living Conditions: Presumably the Toy Poodle has
the same character traits as the larger versions of the Poodle
(see pages 159, 161, and 211). When you buy a puppy, you
should know the breeder, check pedigrees, and place lots of
emphasis on healthy breeding.

Health: Atopic dermatitis, achondroplasia (cartilage abnormalities), osteogenesis imperfecta, PRA, epilepsy, behavioral
abnormalities, lacrimal duct atresia, microphthalmia, cataracts,
patellar luxation, entropion, Legg-Perthes' disease, numerous
cardiac conditions, glaucoma, and Cushing's syndrome.

Appropriate for: Beginners

QUICK INFO FIC Group 9/No. 172: *Companion and Toy
Dogs* **Country of Origin:** *France* **Size:** *10 inches (25 cm)*
Weight: *under 11 pounds (5 kg)* **Fur:** *should be double,
abundant, woolly, and well curled* **Color:** *black, white,
brown, silver, apricot* **Life Expectancy:** *over 10 years*

Weimaraner

History: The Weimaraner is a uniquely colored, impressive hunting dog that was used for hunting primarily in the area of Weimar/Halle during the eighteenth and nineteenth centuries. This is a tracker, pointer, and retriever rolled into one. Its work after the shot is particularly valued. Today it is fairly rare, since it is not a particularly easy dog to own as a companion.

Character: When this dog is well trained, it is a boon to its family, whom it loves and defends. Untrained dogs are unpredictable.

Living Conditions: This dog needs plenty of leadership training that should be continued throughout its life. Kindness and strict consistency are important.

Health: HD, ear infections, entropion, bloat, undershot jaw, dwarfism, elbow dysplasia.

Appropriate for: Experienced hunters

Training: 🐾 🐾 🐾
City: 🐾 🐾 🐾 🐾
Family: 🐾 🐾 🐾
Care: 🐾 🐾
Activity Level: 🐾 🐾 🐾 🐾 🐾

QUICK INFO FIC Group 7/No. 99: *Pointers* **Country of Origin:** *Germany* **Size:** *22–27.5 inches (57–70 cm)* **Weight:** *approximately 66 pounds (30 kg)* **Fur:** *short, thick, fine, shiny or longhaired version* **Color:** *mouse, silver, or deer gray* **Life Expectancy:** *12 to 13 years*

Welsh Corgi Cardigan

Training: 🐾 🐾
City: 🐾
Family: 🐾
Care: 🐾 🐾
Activity Level: 🐾 🐾 🐾

History: A lay person can scarcely distinguish between a Welsh Corgi Cardigan and a Welsh Corgi Pembroke, but they are separate breeds. The Cardigan is considerably longer, but many Pembrokes are born with a shortened tail. Both are watchful, excellent watchdogs, as well as herders of sheep and cattle. The dogs nip them in the heels and avoid getting kicked only because of their small size.

Character: These dogs are self-assured, ambitious, and love games. They continually try to assert themselves. Both breeds require consistent training.

Living Conditions: The Corgi is a natural heeler and will gently herd people, sheep, or ducks, or any other group it finds. In the United States this dog is owned by many who have small children and they are considered excellent companion pets.

Health: A robust, healthy dog.

Appropriate for: Experienced owners

QUICK INFO FIC Group 1/No. 38 (Cardigan), No. 39 (Pembroke): *Sheepdogs and Cattledogs* **Country of Origin:** *Great Britain* **Size:** *10–12.5 inches (25–32 cm)* **Weight:** *Cardigan: 24–37.5 pounds (11–17 kg); Pembroke: 22–26 pounds (10–12 kg)* **Fur:** *smooth, harsh, with soft undercoat* **Color:** *all colors, but white should not predominate* **Life Expectancy:** *12 to 14 years*

Welsh Terrier

History: This dog looks a lot like the Airedale Terrier (see page 30), but this breed is even older. Before it was retrained as a companion dog, the Welsh Terrier drove the fox out of its burrow for the pack of hunting dogs.

Training: 🐾🐾
City: 🐾🐾
Family: 🐾
Care: 🐾🐾🐾🐾
Activity Level: 🐾🐾🐾🐾

It is less contentious than other Terriers. Today it still proves its worth in combating vermin.

Character: This dog is lively, courageous, and adventurous. Sometimes it is balky, but it responds well to training. In its family it is merry and lovable. It is alert, but does not bark excessively.

Living Conditions: Because this dog is very intelligent, it needs adequate games to keep it busy and develop its mind. Agility and competitive dog sports are good choices and absolutely necessary for its physical fitness. It needs active, athletic people who can provide it with action.

Health: No particular known diseases.

Appropriate for: Beginners

QUICK INFO FIC Group 3/No. 78: *Terriers* **Country of Origin:** *Great Britain* **Size:** *15 inches (39 cm)* **Weight:** *19–22 pounds (9–10 kg)* **Fur:** *stiff, wiry, thick topcoat; needs trimming* **Color:** *black and tan or grizzled black* **Life Expectancy:** *up to 14 years*

West Highland White Terrier

Also: *Westie*

Training:	🐾 🐾
City:	🐾
Family:	🐾
Care:	🐾 🐾 🐾 🐾
Activity Level:	🐾 🐾 🐾

History: The blossom-white Westie came about from the Cairn Terrier in the middle of the nineteenth century because the favorite dog of the Malcolm family of Poltalloch was mistaken for a fox and shot. Starting in 1970 the Westie suddenly became so fashionable that even unscrupulous propagators were able to make a killing.

Character: This little, continually comical, self-assured dog has a big personality. In contrast to other Terriers, it shows almost no aggressiveness. It has good endurance and is not bashful.

Living Conditions: This is an ideal house and family dog. Its occasional stubbornness is redeemed by its special charm. Look for the highest quality breeder at time of purchase.

Health: Dislocated knee, allergies, jaw abnormalities, liver diseases, Legg-Perthes' disease, copper toxicosis, HD, deafness.

Appropriate for: Beginners

QUICK INFO FIC Group 3/No. 85: *Terriers* **Country of Origin:** *Great Britain* **Size:** *11 inches (28 cm)* **Weight:** *15–22 pounds (7–10 kg)* **Fur:** *hard, straight, wiry, with soft undercoat; needs trimming* **Color:** *pure white* **Life Expectancy:** *up to 15 years*

West Siberian Laika

Also: *Zapadno-Sibirskaia Laika*

History: This is the most popular of the Laika breeds, which was used primarily for hunting elk, reindeer, and bear. In contrast to the other Laikas, which were used only for hunting, the West Siberian Laika also performed well as a sled dog and could pull heavy loads. These dogs were also used for medical experiments in the Soviet Union. It became famous as the first dog launched into outer space.

Character: Like all Laikas, this dog is robust and spirited and has good endurance. It is primitive in its behavior.

Living Conditions: Individual fanatics for this breed now and again own a Laika. But they are not likely to succeed as companion dogs.

Health: Very robust and healthy.

Appropriate for: Specialists

Training: 🐾 🐾 🐾
City: 🐾 🐾 🐾 🐾
Family: 🐾 🐾 🐾 🐾 🐾
Care: 🐾 🐾
Activity Level: 🐾 🐾 🐾 🐾 🐾

QUICK INFO FIC Group 5/No. 306: *Spitz and Primitive Types* **Country of Origin:** *Russia* **Size:** *21–24 inches (53–61 cm)* **Weight:** *40–51 pounds (18–23 kg)* **Fur:** *thick, coarse guard hairs with heavy undercoat* **Color:** *white, salt and pepper, all shades of red and gray, black, all one color or mottled* **Life Expectancy:** *10 to 12 years*

Whippet

History: Rabbit hunting was very popular in northern England in the nineteenth century. Since the Terriers used for the purpose were still too slow for the sporty English, they crossed them with fairly small greyhounds. This resulted in the maneuverable, lightning-quick Whippet. This breed was also the racing dog of the poor working class of the northern English counties.

Training:	🐾 🐾
City:	🐾 🐾
Family:	🐾
Care:	🐾
Activity Level:	🐾 🐾 🐾 🐾 🐾

Character: As a housemate and companion dog, the Whippet is calm, gentle, and pleasant. It likes close physical contact and is very devoted, but it is never obtrusive. Rolled up into a little ball, it fits on the tiniest couch. It gets along fine with other dogs.

Living Conditions: Since this dog is very active and loves to run and play outdoors, it needs plenty of opportunities to burn off calories. Because of its pronounced hunting instinct, this should take place only in a fenced area. This dog is a good candidate for agility.

Health: No particular diseases.

Appropriate for: Beginners

QUICK INFO **FIC Group 10/No. 162:** *Sighthounds*
Country of Origin: *Great Britain* **Size:** *17–20 inches (43–50 cm)*
Weight: *20–26.5 pounds (9–12 kg)* **Fur:** *short and fine*
Color: *all colors* **Life Expectancy:** *rarely over 15 years*

White Swiss Shepherd

Formerly: *American-Canadian White Shepherd*

History: In the time around 1898, there were some white dogs in the pedigree of Horand von Grafrath, the first German Shepherd entered into the registry. A few breeders in America specialized in this color variant. The "white" passed through Switzerland and also became widespread in Germany

Character: In its disposition, this dog is practically identical to the German Shepherd (see page 112). Overall, though, it is a bit gentler and more sensitive. Its fighting spirit and toughness are somewhat reduced, and that doesn't hurt it as a companion dog. Its inborn defensive instinct is adequate and needs no extra encouragement.

Living Conditions: A versatile candidate for dog sports and as a companion dog. With gentle, consistent training, it is an excellent family dog.

Health: HD, allergies, also see German Shepherd.

Appropriate for: Beginners

Training: 🐾
City: 🐾 🐾 🐾
Family: 🐾
Care: 🐾 🐾
Activity Level: 🐾 🐾 🐾 🐾

QUICK INFO FIC Group 11/No. 347: *Provisionally Recognized Breeds* **Country of Origin:** *Switzerland* **Size:** *22–26 inches (56–66 cm)* **Weight:** *59–86 pounds (27–39 kg)* **Fur:** *double coat with undercoat, rarely long double coat* **Color:** *white* **Life Expectancy:** *approximately 12 years*

Wolf Spitz (Keeshond)

Also: *German Wolf Spitz*

History: In the opinion of well-known cynologists, the Dutch Keeshond and the Wolf Spitz are identical. In Holland this dog was considered a people's dog, in contrast to the noble dog breeds for the upper classes. It got its name in the eighteenth century, when a Dutch patriot named Kees chose this dog as a mascot. In some countries this is a rare breed.

Character: This is a very good watchdog with an inborn defense instinct. You have to use lots of patience with it, but it's worth it. The Wolf Spitz may not tolerate children.

Living Conditions: Since this dog rarely runs after game, it's a good dog to keep in areas that are rich in wild game. It likes to be outdoors. It doesn't tolerate other dogs in its territory.

Health: Epilepsy, heart defects, hypothyroidism.

Appropriate for: Beginners

Training: 🐾 🐾 🐾
City: 🐾 🐾 🐾
Family: 🐾 🐾 🐾
Care: 🐾 🐾 🐾
Activity Level: 🐾 🐾 🐾

QUICK INFO FIC Group 5/No. 97: *Spitz and Primitive Types*
Country of Origin: *Germany* **Size:** *18–24 inches (45–60 cm)*
Weight: *59–81 pounds (27–37 kg)* **Fur:** *long, abundant, thick undercoat* **Color:** *silver gray with black hair tips, black muzzle*
Life Expectancy: *12 to 14 years*

Xoloitzcuintle

Also: *Mexican Hairless*

History: This dog existed as long ago as the early sixteenth century, when the Spaniards conquered Mexico. It served the Aztecs as a living hot water bottle, and they treasured its meat as a table delicacy and sacrificed it to their gods. This dog's physique is similar to that of the greyhounds. The hairless skin requires special care. This breed exists in large (standard), medium (middle variety), and miniature versions.

Training: 🐾 🐾
City: 🐾
Family: 🐾
Care: 🐾
Activity Level: 🐾 🐾 🐾

Character: This is a lively, intelligent, loving dog. It is friendly toward strangers, and neither aggressive nor shy.

Living Conditions: Even though this dog has no hair, it tolerates cold temperatures as long as it can keep moving. It needs extensive walks, for it is very athletic and untiring. This is a good dog for houses with central heat, and for people with allergies to dog hair.

Health: Missing teeth and bite abnormalities.

Appropriate for: Experienced owners

QUICK INFO FIC Group 5/No. 234: *Spitz and Primitive Types* **Country of Origin:** *Mexico* **Size:** *17–22.5 inches (41–57 cm)* **Weight:** *20–31 pounds (9–14 kg)* **Fur:** *hairless* **Color:** *in winter, light gray or pink, in summer dark brown to black* **Life Expectancy:** *12 to 15 years*

Yorkshire Terrier

History: Originally this dog was used to eliminate rats in the narrow, dirty tunnels in the coal mines. Nowadays it is especially admired in dog shows.

Training: 🐾 🐾 🐾
City: 🐾
Family: 🐾
Care: 🐾 🐾 🐾 🐾
Activity Level: 🐾 🐾 🐾

Character: This is a lionhearted dog in a small package! Most Yorkies simply don't understand that they don't even weigh nine pounds (4 kg), and in their delusions of grandeur they even chase away oversized mastiffs.

Living Conditions: If these dogs are not socialized to other dogs when they are puppies, they often act very antisocial in public. Sometimes this behavior may be quite costly in terms of veterinary bills.

Health: Diseases of the retina, dry eye (inadequate tear production), dislocated kneecap and elbow, fontanelle (openings in the bones of the skull), collapse of air passages, Legg-Perthes' disease, kidney stones, liver diseases.

Appropriate for: Beginners

QUICK INFO FIC Group 3/No. 86: *Terriers* **Country of Origin:** *Great Britain* **Size:** *7 inches (18 cm)* **Weight:** *approximately 6.6 pounds (3 kg)* **Fur:** *long, fine, straight* **Color:** *dark steel-blue with full, light tan on breast, head, and legs* **Life Expectancy:** *up to 14 years*

Choosing a Dog

Love for a dog shouldn't be the only motivation for bringing a four-legged companion into the house. In the following chapter you will find the things you should consider before you get a dog.

The Dog's Role In Society

The former situation: The living conditions of our hunter and gatherer ancestors approximated the habits of the wolves. Both were constantly on the search for food and had to defend their territory against intruders. After taming and domestication, dogs could follow people with the same interests. They experienced greater success by cooperating on the hunt. They fit well together because they were able to satisfy similar inclinations.

The situation today: Modern-day humans have moved away from nature. Therefore, they often don't understand dogs. Innate hunting activity is seen as an undesirable behavior problem. Whereas the dog lived around the clock with our forefathers, nowadays it accompanies us only in our free time. But even then it can't be with us all the time. The dog doesn't understand that, for it is a dog the whole day long, and it can't be turned on and off. It also doesn't know the difference between work and play. In addition, its activities in today's society have nothing to do with the dog's conception of work. People need dogs today for abstract social purposes: a substitute for a partner, a child, or a sibling, a leisure time companion, a "device" for sports and games, or a status symbol. In all of these new tasks for dogs there is a great danger of anthropomorphizing them. This is one of the major problems in modern society with dog ownership. The needs of the dog are not met in such humanized person-dog relationships, and that's a setup for problem behavior. The dog doesn't find its role in the family if it doesn't receive

Common experiences are important for a dog's development.

Considerations Prior to Purchase
Before you think about buying a dog, you need to have a love of animals and plenty of knowledge about what dogs need. The dog suffers most when it is expected to think and reason and act like us. So before you buy a dog, always consider, "Why do I want a dog?" Everyone in the family has to be in agreement about the purchase.

kindness and consistent training. Without training it may reverse roles with family members and become the leader, much to the family's dismay. Millions of such dogs end up in animal shelters every year or fill up the cash registers of animal psychologists or the like. Dog sports without pressure to perform, such as agility and competitive events, are a good substitute activity for today's unemployed dogs.

What Do People Expect from Dogs?

For many people it would be great if they could turn the dog on and off. After their free-time fun, they could store the dog next to

the surfboard in the garage, without any pangs of conscience, until it's time to do something else with it. The dog has to meet all of our expectations. However, this usually goes against its needs and its inborn instincts. It must guard, but do nothing against friends, neighbors, and children, even if they annoy it. It mustn't fight with other dogs, and yet it should win if attacked. On a walk, it should burn off steam, but not chase after wild animals. And if it follows its own interests for a distance, it must come back immediately on command. When it wrongly pulls on the leash,

> **Most dogs are as fascinated with water as children are.**

EXTRA TIP

What You Need to Know

Before you get a dog, you absolutely must find out all you can about the biological background and knowledge concerning the appropriate demands that a dog will pose. Good clubs and good private dog schools offer regular theoretical courses. See the checklist on the next page for some important topics!

it is taken off the leash so it can run around free, even though it is not yet trained. Outdoors it is permitted to dig holes, but not in the yard. We expect the dog to be clean and scarcely give it an opportunity to learn housebreaking. We offer it unsavory things to eat, but we don't understand that by nature it is a carrion eater. We expect it to understand our speech, but take no pains to learn its body language. We don't want it to beg, and yet we feed it from the table. When we greet it, we encourage it to jump up on us wildly, but we don't want that to happen with strangers. People nowadays don't need dogs as helpers, but rather as free-time companions. But it doesn't work for the dog to be available whenever the person wishes, and just hang around at other times, without leading to problems.

How People Regard Dogs Today

Dogs have had to give up a lot in their new duties in today's society, which lie almost exclusively in the social realm. They can no longer hunt to earn their living together with humans. Their food is in the dish punctually. They no longer have to fight for a female,

Playing with a Frisbee is a substitute for thwarted hunting pleasure.

> **A dog needs to learn pleasure-oriented games early on.**

which now is provided. The original purpose for which the dog was bred is not even known to many people. Even former work dogs such as the German Shepherd today are overloaded with luxury as pure family dogs. They are unemployed—and they suffer. They merely get taken on unimaginative walks a couple of times a day. They have no real tasks anymore that require them to use their inbred intelligence. That's why today's dogs are often hyperactive, unsatisfied, frustrated, and ultimately ill behaved. Naturally, dogs have a need for exercise, but like wolves they don't want to work it off through mindless running. An animal's exercise is

always directed toward a meaningful activity. Dogs spontaneously do things on walks that partially satisfy them and keep the boring walks from becoming totally stultifying. They continually go farther away from their pack leader and follow their interest in hunting. Humans have forgotten their cooperation with dogs, but the dogs are not satisfied with the role that has been assigned to them. Because of

EXTRA TIP

How to Make a Walk More Fun

Make the walk like a hunting adventure. Always go different routes that your dog isn't familiar with. Give it various tasks that it enjoys because it can master them. Choose games and activities that are fun. It doesn't matter what you do; the dog is happy whenever it can do it with you.

> **Even heavy, massive dogs occasionally show ambition for the hunt.**

their social behavior and structure, dogs have chosen to live with humans ever since primeval times. They want to experience things together when they leave their "den." That can happen only through thoughtful activity, however, when the humans understand their dogs' needs.

The Unknowing Human From a Dog's Viewpoint

Everything that we do in the presence of a dog gets recorded and judged. That has an effect on such things as who is the leader of the pack in the future. Our behavior is a decisive factor in what kind of image the dog has of us. The regular walk shows the dog every day that we are not suited for the hunt. Through various canine gestures and body language it continually tries to invite us to go hunting together—until it gives

> **Combative games must remain under the control of the human.**

up and follows its own interests alone. It does the same thing in playing. That's how it lays claim to the rights of the higher rank. But we are proud that the dog brings us a toy as an invitation to play and barks a command to throw the ball. We become a ball-throwing machine under the dog's control.

When a dog jumps onto the couch and the human moves over to make room, the dog becomes convinced that it deserves that spot as a superior in the pecking order. When the dog is allowed to defend the front door after someone knocks, the human acknowledges the dog as a superior and the responsible party at this important territorial boundary. Later on, the dog will not be enthused about disputing this position with a person of lower caste. There can be some serious and even dangerous misun-

Even a "little squirt" knows the body language for inviting someone to play.

derstandings because of these human errors, which allow the dog to develop the conviction that it is the boss. The human grants the dog liberties appropriate to a pack leader, but the dog is supposed to be submissive in certain situations. But a grown dog will defend its elevated status with bared teeth in an effort to discipline the "disobedient one."

The Definition of a Dog

It could read as follows: This is an instinct driven predator that likes to run, and which lives in a hierarchical social arrangement.

The collection of its instincts, its physical constitution, and its sense organs are set up for successful hunting. As early as their puppy days, our dogs practice complete hunting sequences, including the kill. This includes stalking, fixating on the prey, hunting, pouncing, playful biting, and pulling down. At the same time, during the imprinting phase, these games help lay the foundation for getting along with

EXTRA TIP

Establishing the Hierarchy
In order to gain recognition as a superior from a dog, you must avoid making mistakes according to its standards. Thus, the dog should not precede you through doors, on stairs, or on a leash. In playing, clearly establish the beginning and the end of the game. In walking, you set the direction and the pace. Through your activities, you keep the dog from being concerned only with its own interests.

other dogs later in life. Dogs come into the world with their inborn instincts, which should be the basis for their learning. They really don't need many of their instincts anymore, for much of their natural behavior is no longer desirable, and it even leads to problems. Every type of behavior that a dog displays is appropriate to its kind. To keep it from displaying it in the wrong time and place, it needs firm training. That encourages wanted behavior and discourages undesirable behavior. But people who love dogs will accept them just as they are, with their overall behavior and their ways.

CHECKLIST

What Dogs Are and What They Want

- ✔ They are quick to perceive movement, and are thus good hunters.
- ✔ They don't like to be left alone.
- ✔ Their sense of smell is infinitely better than that of humans.
- ✔ They are dependent upon people and very adaptable.
- ✔ They need meaningful activity and not just a chance to run free.

Always bear to the left when meeting other walkers.

EXTRA TIP

Dogs Are Hunters

Even today, a dog's anatomy and behavior are tuned to hunting for prey. Its instincts include hunting, the pack, sex, and territory.

Its sense organs, which in performance far exceed human ones (with the exception of taste), correspond to smell, hearing, and movement perception. These are the sense organs of an exceptional hunter.

Scuffing after urinating heightens the marking effect.

Getting the Right Dog

In the Extra Tip on page 231 we asked the question, "Why do I want a dog?" If the family is in agreement on that point, the next very important question is, "Which dog is the right choice for us?" In choosing a breed, you shouldn't be guided primarily by the dog's appearance. You have to pay much more attention to the sum of its character traits, its breed-specific purpose, required living conditions, future size, its life expectancy, trainability, its suitability to the family, and its need for exercise. Since

Among dogs, this behavior means, "So who are you?"

every dog presents breed-specific demands, it falls to us to determine if we can satisfy these demands. We have to consider that we will

239

live with this dog for some twelve to fifteen years. If you make the wrong choice, that can be a very long time, and bring lasting problems. The fact that nearly a third of all dog owners experience fairly serious problems because the dog is not the right fit proves that many people who buy dogs disregard these considerations.

Not even canine psychologists can reliably cure the inborn, individual characteristics of breeds that don't meet people's expectations. And that is the start of a long road of discomfort, often for both parties, and thousands of dogs end up in animal shelters every year.

Look before you leap...
➤ Are my family, financial, and professional relations set up in such a way that the living conditions for the dog will remain the same for twelve to fifteen years?

➤ Do I have the right temperament for a "lively" dog?
➤ Do I have the time and the right conditions to jog or ride a bike every day with a dog that likes to run?
➤ Am I ready to have fewer and fewer friends visit because of an aggressive watchdog?
➤ Do I have the physical strength to assert my dominance on the street if the dog grows up to weigh twenty pounds more than I do?
➤ Am I allowed to keep a dog in the house I rent?

Finding the Right Puppy

Once you decide on a specific breed, you need to locate a good breeder.

Requirements for Breeders
The breeder should be associated with a national breed association (see Addresses, page 255), and be involved in breeding for love of animals, and not for reasons of profit. The breeder should have waiting lists of people

Extreme hunting behavior is undesirable in a companion dog.

Getting the Right Advice

Get some advice from a dog expert to help you choose the right breed. That should be someone who knows several breeds. Ask a veterinarian or get information from good dog schools whose trainers naturally deal with many different breeds. Breeders and owners of specific breeds will nearly always praise and extol *their* breed.

who want puppies and pester you with all kinds of questions to be sure that you are the right person for the puppy. If that breeder's prices seem higher than someone else's who is advertising puppies in the paper, don't think about the money. When you buy a dog, bargains are often more expensive in the end.

Finding the Right Breeder:
Veterinarians and good dog schools generally can recommend good breeders. You can also find links to breeders at dog association websites. If you get a recommendation to a breeder from an unknown source, get some information about the person from the local animal shelter. If you don't have

1 Attentive

2 Curiosity Cubed

3 An enthusiastic welcome encourages the dog to come.

4 Nose Training

Playful Pups **5**

much experience with dogs, ask an expert to go with you when you buy a puppy. Even if you have to pay for the service, that person's help can save you lots of aggravation and money. There are, unfortunately, some black sheep in this business who recognize a novice right away and take advantage of the person's inexperience. Never buy a sick or poorly bred dog out of pity. Make the purchase contract contingent on an examination of the puppy by a veterinarian.

The Costs of Keeping a Dog

Before you buy a dog, think about all the consequences of that purchase. The following questions should help you decide.

➤ Do you have enough room, and hopefully a yard, for the dog? Many breeds are unsuited for indoor living only.

➤ Do you have the time to take two to three walks with the dog every day, even in bad weather?

➤ Can you guarantee that the dog will be left alone no longer than several hours at a stretch during the day?

➤ Do you have the time required for training, further development, and athletic activities with your dog?

➤ Are you willing to plan your vacation so that you can take your dog along? Or is there someone the dog trusts who can take care of it when you are on vacation or ill?

➤ Are you prepared to pay the costs associated with food, care, dog registration, and liability insurance?

➤ Are all family members in agreement about buying a dog?

EXTRA TIP

The Right Puppy

1. It should be no older than eight to ten weeks, and be imprinted on humans.
2. It must be wormed and have the appropriate shots for its age (shot record).
3. A healthy puppy's fur, mouth, eyes, nose, ears, and bottom are clean.
4. It is attentive to the things going on around it and accepts an invitation to play.

➤ Is anyone in the family allergic to dog hair? If you're not sure, you should check with a doctor before getting a dog.

➤ Have you come to an agreement with your family about who is going to be the main reference person for the dog? Every dog, especially the working breeds, needs a person that it recognizes as the "leader of the pack," and on whom it focuses. This person must take over the basic and subsequent training.

Interesting walks for dogs take up a lot of time.

➤ Are you able, from professional and private viewpoints, to plan over a period of around twelve years (the dog's presumed lifespan)?

➤ Does your landlord allow dogs?

➤ Are you willing to take the time and pay the costs associated with bringing your dog to a veterinarian for regular checkups and necessary vaccinations?

> Think of your dogs'
> needs when you take
> long trips by car.

What a Dog Costs
The financial outlay for a medium-sized dog with a life
expectancy of around twelve years involves purchase, food,
care, veterinary bills (without particular illnesses), registration fees, and insurance to the tune of around $12,000.
The yearly membership fee for a dog club is about another
$50 to $70. Dog training courses cost from $100 to $150.
You can spend up to three hours two to three times a week
doing sports with the dog at a club.

Illnesses from
A to Z

➤ **Albinism**
Hereditary lack of pigmentation in the skin, eyes, and
hair. Affected animals are
usually sensitive to sunlight.

➤ **Anemia**
Reduced amount of hemo-
globin in the bloodstream
caused by production failure,
reduction of red blood cells,
or decreased volume of blood
caused by internal or external
hemorrhage.

➤ **Anthropomorphism**
The attributing of human
characteristics to an animal.
Considering your dog as
a human member of the
family.

➤ **Atopy**
Often hereditary
predisposition to
skin allergies
resulting in
itching, scratch-
ing, skin inflam-
mation.

➤ **Autoimmune disease**
Production of antibodies that
attack and damage living cells
within the body.

➤ **Blood clotting failures**
Platelet insufficiency due to
blood protein defects.

➤ **Blue Doberman syndrome**
Hereditary pigment dilution
that causes thin, fragile skin,
coats, and eyes in the Doberman Pinscher.

➤ **Cervical myelopathy**
Disease of the spinal cord in
the cervical or neck region.

➤ **Cleft Palate**
Fissure of the hard palate or
roof of the mouth caused by
failure of the two halves of
the palate to unite during
prenatal development.

➤ **Collapsed windpipe**
Softening of cartilage rings
and lengthening of ligaments
of the trachea, causing
collapse. May be surgically
repaired.

➤ **Collie nose**
Hereditary lack of pigment in
the dorsum of the muzzle of
Collies and Shelties that may
be associated with autoimmune disease. The tissue
becomes sunburned with
consequent sloughing of skin.

➤ **Copper poisoning**
Occurs because of hereditary
failure of copper metabolism
and retention of copper in
the body.

➤ **Cryptorchidism**
Failure of both testicles to descend normally into the scrotum. Failure of one testicle to properly descend is called monorchidism.

➤ **Cushing's disease or hyperadrenalcorticism**
Thought to be hereditary. A syndrome that is brought about by excess amounts of cortisone-like chemicals in the bloodstream causing weight gain, skin disease, and general malaise.

➤ **Diabetes Mellitus**
An often hereditary condition caused by degeneration or defect in the pancreas wherein insulin production is insufficient and glucose is retained in the bloodstream and excreted into the urine.

➤ **Double teeth**
Failure of baby (deciduous) teeth to be shed on time resulting in a double set of teeth. Food and hair are often trapped between the rows of teeth causing problems.

➤ **Dystocia**
Difficulty whelping. Any of the many problems when giving birth to a normal litter.

➤ **Eclampsia**
Inadequate blood calcium metabolism at or near whelping that causes the bitch to become nervous and uncoordinated, and eventually results in staggering, convulsions, coma, and death.

➤ **Ectasia**
Hereditary Collie and Sheltie eye syndrome in which retinal degeneration progresses from birth to eventually result in blindness at varying ages.

➤ **Elbow dysplasia**
Hereditary deformity of the ulna bone that forms part of the elbow joint.

➤ **Ectropion**
Hereditary excess skin of the face causing a predisposition for the eyelids to sag and droop and expose the sensitive mucous membranes to irritation.

➤ **Entropion**
Hereditary predisposition of the upper or lower eyelids or both, to roll inward causing the lashes to irritate the cornea and cause ulceration.

➤ **Hemophilia A**
Hereditary blood clotting failure caused by defect in blood protein and subsequent lack of platelet formation.

➤ **Hip dysplasia (HD)**
Deformity of head of the femur and the socket (acetabulum) in the pelvic bone that progresses from birth until old age and results in arthritic pain and sometimes the inability to rise from a lying position.

➤ **Hookworm**
An endoparasite that fastens to the lining of a dog's intestine and can cause internal hemorrhage.

➤ **Hypersialosis**
Drooling that can be a hereditary condition in Newfoundlands or Saint Bernards.

➤ **Hypoglycemia**
Hereditary predisposition to lowered blood sugar that in turn causes lowered body temperature, fatigue, reduced mental alertness, and paralysis.

➤ **Hypothryoidism**
Often hereditary reduction of production of thyroid gland hormones. Often results in obesity and skin diseases among others.

➤ **Impetigo**
Disease of puppies manifested by blisters and brown crusts on the abdomen.

➤ **Inguinal hernia**
Hernia of the groin that may be congenital.

➤ **KCS**
Abbreviation for keratoconjunctivitis sicca, a dry-eye syndrome sometimes caused by insufficiency of tear secretion.

➤ **Legg-Perthes-Calvé disease**
Hereditary and spontaneous degeneration of the uppermost portion of the femur (femoral head). Especially important in small dogs. Onset is about six months of age.

➤ **Lens luxation**
Dislocation of the optic lens that typically occurs as dogs get older; also known as a senile cataract.

➤ **Lip-fold dermatitis**
Skin infection typically found in breeds that have folded or wrinkled flews; it often results from the continual dampness in the deep folds of the skin.

➤ **Luxated patella**
The patella (knee cap) dislocation caused by a hereditarily shallower than normal groove in the patella in which the patella slides. Hereditary weak ligaments that fail to hold the patella in place.

➤ **Lyme disease**
A tick-borne disease that causes joint inflammation, arthritis, and general malaise.

➤ **Mange**
Infestation of ectoparasites: specifically, mites. This skin disorder causes redness and scaly, itchy lesions.

➤ **Microphthalmia**
Hereditarily small and non-functional or abnormally formed eyeball. The dog often is blind at birth.

➤ **Osteochondritis dessicans (OCD)**
Developmental disease that is seen mostly in the shoulder joints of puppies of large breeds.

➤ **Progressive Retinal Atrophy (PRA)**
Hereditary and progressive deterioration of the central portion of the retina of the eye causing a reduced ability to see fixed objects.

➤ **Rage syndrome**
Genetic predisposition to sudden violent tantrums during which a dog may attack inanimate objects or other dogs, even owners. Occasionally seen in Cockers and Springers.

➤ **Rickets**
Bone disease found in puppies caused by improper nutrition or mineral imbalance.

➤ **Ringworm**
A skin disease caused by a fungus.

➤ **Slipped disc syndrome**
The intervertebral disc is a cartilage ring filled with a gelatinous mass that protects the spinal cord as it extends down the center of the verte-brae from the brain to the tail bone. If the disc slips or if it ruptures and its contents flow into the spinal canal, the result is pressure on the spinal cord, resulting in partial paralysis (paresis) or total paralysis.

➤ **Tetany**
Muscle twitching, spasm, or even convulsion.

➤ **von Willebrand's disease**
Genetic mutation causing defect in blood protein which causes bleeding or clotting disorders, brought about by inbreeding.

➤ **Zoonosis**
A disease of animals that can be transmitted to humans, such as rabies.

Breed Index

Page numbers in **bold print** refer to illustrations.

Subject Index

Addresses

Associations and Clubs

American Kennel Club
5880 Centerview Drive,
Suite 200
Raleigh, NC 27606-3390
919-233-9780

The Canadian Kennel Club
100-89 Skyway Avenue
Etobicoke, Ontario M9W6R4
Canada
416-675-5511

American Field Publishing
Company
542 South Dearborn Street
Chicago, IL 60605
312-663-9797

American Rare Breeds
Association
9921 Frank Tippett Road
Cheltenham, MD 20623
301-868-5718

United Kennel Club
100 E. Kilgore Road
Kalamazoo, MI 49002-5584
616-343-9020

Insurances

Check with your insurance
company; some offer liability
insurance for dog owners, and
even health insurance for pets.

Dog Registry

You can protect your dog from
animal thieves and death in a
research laboratory by entering
it into a dog registry. Entry and
computer-assisted search upon
report of a missing dog are free.

Helpful Periodicals

AKC Gazette
Subscriptions: 919-233-9767

Dog Fancy
P.O. Box 53264
Boulder, CO 80322-3264

Dog World
29 North Wacker Drive
Chicago, IL 60606

Off-Lead
204 Lewis Street
Canastota, NY 13032
800-241-7619

Helpful Books

American Kennel Club. *The Complete Dog Book.* New York, New York: Howell Book House, 1992.

Ammen, Amy. *Training in No Time: An Expert's Approach to Effective Dog Training for Hectic Life Styles.* New York, New York: Howell Book House, 1995.

Bailey, Gwen. *The Well-behaved Dog.* Hauppauge, New York: Barron's Educational Series, Inc., 1988.

Ludwig, Gerd. *My Dream Dog.* Hauppauge, New York: Barron's Educational Series, Inc., 2001.

——. *Sit! Stay! Train Your Dog the Easy Way.* Hauppauge, New York: Barron's Educational Series, Inc., 1998.

Smith, Cheryl S. *Pudgy Pooch, Picky Pooch.* Hauppauge, New York: Barron's Educational Series, Inc., 1998.

Taunton, Stephanie J. and Cheryl S. Smith. *The Trick Is in the Training.* Hauppauge, New York: Barron's Educational Series, Inc., 1998.

Cover Photo: Kromfohrlander; **Back Cover:** Longhaired Collie (top), Berger de Brie (middle), Beagle (bottom)

The Photographers

Bilder Pur/Klein, Hubert; Bilder Pur/Steimer; Cogis/Alexis; Cogis/DR; Cogis/Français; Cogis/Gauzargue; Cogis/Hermeline; Cogis/Labat; Cogis/Lanceau; Cogis/Niçaise; Cogis/Simon; Cogis/Vedie; Juniors/Botzenhardt; Juniors/Brinkmann; Juniors/Cherek; Juniors/Essler; Juniors/Farkaschovsky; Juniors/Freiburg; Juniors/Köpfle; Juniors/Krämer; Juniors/Kuczka; Juniors/Naroska; Juniors/Prawitz; Juniors/Schanz; Juniors/Stuewer; Juniors/Wegler; Juniors/Wegner; Krämer; Layer; Raab; Reinhard; Schanz; Silvestris/Lenz; Silvestris/Sunset; Steimer; Wegler

English translation copyright © 2005 by Barron's Educational Series, Inc.

Published originally under the title *Hunderassen von A bis Z*
Copyright © 2003 by Gräfe und Unzer Verlag GmbH, Munchen

English translation by Eric A. Bye, M.A.

All inquiries should be addressed to:
Barron's Educational Series, Inc.
250 Wireless Boulevard
Hauppauge, NY 11788
www.barronseduc.com

International Standard Book No. 0-7641-3057-9

Library of Congress Catalog Card No. 2004104915

PRINTED IN CHINA

9 8 7 6